One Product Away

Find, Source, and Sell Products With The Foolproof AMZ Formula to Get Rich For Life Selling On Amazon

By Joshua Crisp

INTRODUCTION

I was in a hotel bath robe, nestled in a chaise lounge at the edge of our private infinity pool, with the sun setting over the Indian Ocean. I was loving the laid-back island vibe of the Maldives, although at that moment my focus was on my laptop, resting on the coffee table on the wooden deck that I was using as my new office.

I was looking at my sales figures for just one of the items I was selling on Amazon. It was still bringing me six figures per year for just that one thing.

I didn't make that thing.

I didn't store it.

I didn't ship it.

I didn't even answer the phone if someone had a problem with it.

My only job right now was to enjoy the sea-salty air and the smell of tropical flowers surrounding our private room, along with my wife and sons.

No emails.

No calls.

I didn't even need to check my account balance.

But that night I was smiling. I was so grateful for all this abundance, all this wealth – not just the money but the opportunity to be present in my kids' lives. The chance to have allowed my wife and my mother to retire.

Less than five years earlier, all four of us were all crammed into a 400 square foot apartment that I couldn't afford – even though it was only $375 per month. I was collecting rent voucher checks by volunteering during the daytime at Center Township, volunteering at the Salvation Army to put food on our table.

I went to work the night shift at the recycling plant when my little boys went to sleep, and got back just before they woke up, for $7.25 per hour. It wasn't enough money to support me, let alone a family of four.

It wasn't enough sleep to keep me alive. My heart was constantly racing and I kept thinking I might die of exhaustion. My fingers trembled so bad at work, at home, I could barely get my key into the front door.

I knew something had to change. My circumstances had to change, or I was going to die and leave my wife and kids with nothing but debt. I came from a split family that had nothing and gave me nothing but tough life lessons. There was nobody out there who was going to give me a dollar.

It was me that had to change.

Once I realized that, I was fully committed. If anything was going to change in my life, I was going to have be the one to change it. Armed with one-hundred percent commitment, I set forth to change my legacy in this world.

I wasn't going to die a burnt-out, washed-up loser that nobody cared about. I was going to find a way to take care of myself, my family, and do something that made a difference.

What I didn't know yet, was that I was only one product away from changing everything and living a wildly success-ful, wealthy life.

CHAPTER 1

IT SHOULD NEVER HAVE BEEN ME

"IF you really want to do something, you'll find a way. If you don't, you'll find an excuse"

•*Jim Rohn*

It should never have been me.

I should never have become successful in life.

I should never have made tens of millions of dollars, been completely satisfied and happily married with a wife and two sons, or helped thousands of people from over one hundred countries to find their financial freedom and get rich.

My dad ran out on me. My step-dad was an immigrant. We were poor, marginalized people in a country that couldn't give a rat's ass about us. I had no good role models. My mom loved me, but she worked so hard to keep food on our table that I barely saw her.

I made friends with the wrong crowd because there was nobody else around.

I made bad decisions.

I got kicked out of high school.

I was a felon by the age of 18.

I had no credit, no car, no money, no computer, no fancy phone, no internet.

Every card in the deck was stacked against me, and every person in my life expected me to amount to nothing, so there's no way I should have made anything of myself, let alone become successful at anything.

But I did.

Every one of those details was just an excuse. Every thought in my programming about my being a failure and never amounting to anything was just a shortcut for me to avoid the hard work it would take to turn my life around.

Back then, I didn't even know what I didn't know. Every single detail of how I could work hard to pull myself out of my low position in life was foreign to me. Nobody showed me how to do it. All I saw around me were people struggling to make a living so small and a life so tiny, they were invisible.

I was invisible, just like them. Nobody cares about you when you're nothing.

We were all crabs in a fisherman's bucket. Every time one of us tried to escape the bucket, another crab pulled us back down.

I thought I was supposed to go out and get a good job, but I had no education, no skills, no work experience, and no work references who would say a kind thing about me. I didn't even have nice clothes for a job interview. Nobody in their right mind is going to give you a job when you're that unqualified.

What I did have was a young family, two little boys, an out-of-work, immigrant wife who was focusing on being a full-time mom and homemaker. I had debt that would prob- ably take me the rest of my life to make minimum payments on. I had a 400 square-foot apartment that I couldn't afford, even at only $375 a month.

My One Thing

But I had one thing going for me.

I wanted to change.

I wanted it bad. So bad, I would do anything to change. I knew that somewhere out there was a better life for me, my family, my broke mom and step-dad. There had to be a way to work for it, I just needed to find it.

There were plenty of excuses out there for me to blame my poor circumstances on, like my childhood, my upbringing, my background, my education, my ethnicity, my location, a generational system of oppression that didn't want me to make it. Pick one, they're all a perfectly valid reason why I was where I was.

But that one thing, the desire to change myself and not just make an excuse, made me stand out. I was going to be different. I was different. And the only thing separating me from everyone around was that one thought.

Can you imagine if everybody knew that secret? The only thing that makes any of us different is a single thought?

That's all I had.

That's all I needed.

A Mentor Appears

My mind was made up that I was going to change and get myself out of my own mess. I put that message out into the universe. I put out that energy that I was done being a nobody and I was ready for success.

I had no idea what that even meant at the time, but I was ready to be successful.

Like magic, a mentor appeared. Not some sparkly, fairy-tale nonsense. A real human with a real solution to my problem.

Maybe he was there all along and I just didn't know it. I could have been blind to this opportunity all along because I wasn't committed to myself yet.

Regardless, my eyes were finally open. I was ready for the message.

He said that there was money to be made on Amazon. Anyone with the right mindset, the right tools, and commitment to see it through could make a comfortable living selling on Amazon. Anyone could even get rich if they scaled their business.

Anyone.

Even me.

It was too good to be true. There had to be a catch. There had to be something shady about it. Nobody can just open up a business and make a bunch of money. Maybe trust fund kids who can invest a million dollars first.

But there was no catch. It's just that most people didn't have the right mindset, the right tools, or commitment.

I was ready to give it a try. I thought maybe this was the thing that was going to change my life, because I thought I could do all those things. So I listened. I took notes. I literally wrote pages and pages of notes.

My mentor told me that a sharp pencil is better than a sharp mind. Note takers are money makers – so when you hear something that's going to change your life, write it down.

I took notes on everything he said. I still look back on those notes sometimes, because they were like instructions for printing money.

From that moment on, when I read books, when I listened to audio books, when I watched instructions and tutorials on YouTube, when I do anything where it involves learning, I take notes based off of how I'm actually perceiving what it is that I'm learning, not just notes about what the material said.

You can always go back and re-read, re-listen, or re-watch if you forgot something.

Taking notes involves you in the process. It gets your mind going. It gives you ideas – your own ideas based on what's being presented. It makes the material real to you and relevant to your situation.

Change the way you learn and you will change the way you live.

Write that down.

All In

I was all in. This had to work, or it had to work. There was no other option. There was no going back to the recycling plant to waste my life away late at night while the rest of the world slept.

I was going to become a business man and sell stuff on Amazon.

I was finally going to go to bed like everyone else, but now I was going to make money in my sleep while my business worked for itself.

That's the only way to build true wealth, is to be making money when you're not spending time working. You can trade as many hours as you want for your paycheck, but at the end of the day, every hour you're not working is time you're not getting paid.

I was worth more than the 200 hours per month I was working, which after taxes couldn't even properly feed my family and give us a respectable place to live.

I was worth more than a paper punch-out card that we used to clock in and out to work.

I was worth more than anything anybody every expected

of me, although the bar was set pretty low.

Maybe it should never have been me, and I should never have been successful, but it was me, and I am successful now.

I'm living the life I want to live. I helped retire my wife, my mother, and I only work because I enjoy what I do, which is mostly being a mentor for other people who are struggling.

I brought in eight figures in sales over the last five years and I'm financially set for life, my kids are set for life, and if they have kids, then they're going to be set for life, too.

That's what you can get if you're all in.

I have plenty of everything I ever wanted in life, so the only thing left for me to do is teach others how to do what I did. I want to offer you the opportunity to find out how to change your own life, forever. I want you to find financial freedom and make enough, or make much more than enough if you want.

So if you're all in and you want to make a commitment right now to learn to change your life and your circumstances, then you should keep reading (and taking notes). Otherwise, you should probably stop right here and go back to your old way of life – because anything I say is not going to change you if you don't act on it.

I want you to know that this book alone is enough to help you get started with making a ton of money and completely changing your circumstances. But if for any reason you reach a point where you need a little extra help, please call me at +(512)-548-2467 and I can help you with anything you're stuck on.

The difference between people who get stuck and figure it out themselves and people who ask for help is time. You might find your way eventually, and I hope you do. This book is an excellent resource. But if you want to speed that process up and have me literally hand you a map to success and help you get around your stuck points, call me.

CHAPTER 2

THE ONLY TWO WAYS TO FAIL

"I HAVE NOT FAILED. *I've just found 10,000 ways that don't work.*"

•*Thomas Eddison*

I used to be afraid that if I ever tried to accomplish anything, it wouldn't work. It didn't matter what it was, I was pretty sure that I was bad at everything. No matter what I tried to make happen, I would fail.

Sure enough, that's where I put all my time and energy – thinking about what a failure I was going to be.

My friend told me about a great job opportunity and told me I should apply. I was sure I wasn't qualified, but out of respect for my friend, I went into the store, took a job application and filled it out. When I went back to turn in my job application, the manager wasn't around, so I left it with a cashier at the front of the store.

I never heard back from them, so I assumed they just threw my application away. That proved to me at that time, that I was no good. I sucked. I wasn't worth hiring.

Honestly, I don't even know if the person hiring ever knew I applied for the job. Maybe my application did get thrown away accidentally before they ever saw it. Maybe I was unqualified.

I never followed up. I never called to see if they got the application. I never went back into the store to see if I could set up a meeting with the manager. I never expressed any interest in that job, other than taking five minutes to fill out the application – and my handwriting is pretty bad so even that was a mess.

But that one instance validated the feelings I was already having about myself at the time – that nobody wanted to hire me. That was all in my head.

My friend called me up a week later and asked why I didn't apply. He said they hired the first person who sat down for an interview because they just needed somebody right now.

I felt like an idiot at the time, and I was an idiot at thetime.

Looking back on it, I'm glad I didn't get that job, because JOB stands for Just Over Broke.

At that time, I didn't even think I was qualified to trade the rest of my life away for a pittance, staying broke no matter how many hours I worked.

If I did get that job and worked hard at it, I would have spent about 50 hours a week, 52 weeks a year, or about 2,600 hours of my own life – every single year. All that hard work would be to make somebody else rich, because I was only going to make $18,850 before taxes – that's about $13,195 per year.

That's it.

$13,195 to cover my rent, and food for 4 people. Or, that covers about one trip to the hospital if you don't have insurance.

Even worse than that? I was so hard on myself, I didn't even think I could get that job.

Two Ways To Fail

We may all have a different definition of what it means to be successful, and that's fine. But before you can be successful, you need to mistakes that you can learn from, first.

Let me be clear about the difference between making mistakes you can learn from, and true failure.

There are only two ways that you can fail in life.

1. Don't start
2. Give up

That's it. Any time something doesn't work out the way you expected it to, you can learn from that and try something new next time. You can always pivot, learn, spin, try again.

The only way you actually fail is if you're not brave enough to ever begin, or you quit.

That's all.

Everything else is a mistake that you can learn from and improve on when you don't give up and try it again.

Who This Book Is For

This book is for people who want to use a proven formula to completely change their lives. But it's not just the book that's going to do that. You can't buy anything in this life and expect it to do the work for you.

The information inside this book isn't fool proof, because there are plenty of fools out there who find gems of information and then don't do anything with them.

If you're the type of person who is ready to start a project and will not give up on it, then this book and this system is for you.

Change happens by choice, never by chance. If you knew better, you would do better. This book is to help you know better.

If you read this book and learn these amazing things now and then you don't implement them, you're the one letting yourself and your family down. You're the one that is not breaking that generational curse of poverty.

If you have not come from a wealthy family, you must make a wealthy family come from you. And that will not happen comfortably by just reading a book and expecting results without working for them.

The system right now does not work in your favor to help you make enough money to care for yourself and your family. You're taxed when you buy something, you're taxed when you sell something, you're even taxed when you die.

If you're ready to make enough money to live and thrive, and most importantly to get your time back, then this book is for you. Because time is your most valuable asset. You can never replace it. You can never recreate it. And regardless of how successful you become, you can never buy it. Once it's gone, it's gone.

Who This Book Is Not For

This book is not for people who make POOR decisions, people who are Passing Over Opportunities Repeatedly.

If you're the type of person who gets great advice and

never takes it, or can't be bothered to do any work to improve your own life, then you will get nothing from this book.

Discipline weighs ounces and regret weighs tons. There are plenty of opportunities in this life for everyone, even for the underdogs and the people cast away and marginalized by society.

I have been there. Maybe long ago, this book wasn't even for me because I didn't think I deserved anything good in this world. I didn't believe I was quali ed to do anything. I was laying in my bed, staring at the ceiling fan spinning slowly asking myself, what if I would've made that choice? What if I would've taken action?

That regret is painful. It's real. You feel it for the rest of your life if you constantly miss out on everything because you can't be bothered to do anything.

This book is not for failures, and I don't mean people who make mistakes or who have done some really stupid stuff in their past. I mean people who don't start, they don't act, and then they give up.

This book is not for people who are good at making excuses, unless you're willing to kick those excuses out of your life and finally just commit to something, then follow through.

This book is not for you unless you decide it is. If you really want to change your circumstances, you have to take action and do it. It's as simple as that. Even if you've had things not work out for you in the past, or you've been a failure your whole life.

If you're ready to change, then change. Then, this book is for you.

A Light In The Attic

• • •

Thomas Edison was one of the most famous inventors in

American history. But he wasn't a super genius who just came up with something and it worked on the first try.

The problem he was facing was that he was trying to find the right material to make a filament, the stuff that goes inside of the glass bulb and lights up. There were plenty of promising tries – materials that would glow, but then burn out.

He burnt out dozens, hundreds, and eventually thousands of broken bulbs before he finally found something that worked. He wasn't insane, he could see the value of not giving up and sticking with it because he was working on changing the world.

After almost 10,000 tries, he finally nailed it and invented a light bulb that worked.

Thomas Edison understood that it wasn't a big deal how many times he failed. It was the success that he got at the end, because he started, he worked at it, and he never gave up, that led to his success.

Imagine how the world would be different if Thomas Edison had given up after his first few tries making a light bulb. Maybe we would still be burning whale oil to light our homes today. Or maybe somebody else who started the light bulb project and didn't give up would have been successful, instead of Edison.

CHAPTER 3

MY MILLION DOLLAR MISTAKE

"ANYONE WHO HAS NEVER MADE a mistake has never tried anything new."

• *Albert Einstein*

I didn't start with a million dollars and lose it. I started with nothing and now I make tens of millions of dollars per year. But I made some big mistakes on the way to my own Finan- cial success.

Looking back on it, I'm glad I started at all and kept at it, otherwise, I wouldn't be where I am now. Even knowing that, I could have succeeded faster and better if I had known a few things First.

I want to share these things with you.

You can either learn from the mistakes of others and save yourself time and money, or if you're really committed to doing things the hard way, you can learn from your own mistakes and lose out on your own time and money.

The stuff that I'm sharing with you took several years and dozens of expensive mistakes to learn. I learned the hard way because I didn't have access to the knowledge I'm going to share with you.

The money you can earn back, so in the long run it's not that big a deal, although right now it can sting if you're not at a place where you can lose a lot of money and still make ends meet.

It's time itself that you will never get back. That's the hardest part of any new venture, is trying to gure out how much time you're going to invest, how much time you're going to spend making mistakes you can learn from.

A Chance At Success

Have you ever given something a chance?

You go see a movie with your friend, even though you know you're not going to like it. Five minutes into the movie, you don't like it. You gave it a chance, but it was bad. You know it was bad pretty much right from the beginning.

But did you really give that movie a chance?

Your mind was already made up that you weren't going to like it. Even five minutes in you proved to yourself that you were right and that the movie was bad. You were looking for proof in every part of the movie about how bad it was, so you could not like it.

That's not a chance at all. It's you giving up on something before it's finished.

It's the same way with relationships. If you're looking for things you don't like about the other person, you're going to find them.

It's the same way with business. If you're looking for reasons why your business isn't going to succeed and you should just give up, or switch, you're going to find plenty of reasons.

Excuses.

But if you want something bad enough, even more than excuses, you can stop the excuses and just work on it.

You can nish the movie and then make up your mind.

You can see that the person you're interested in is human, and choose to accept them for who they are and love them unconditionally.

You can choose to stick with your business and watch it succeed – especially if you're on the right path.

You don't want a chance at success. You want a clear, proven path to success. A path that you know that if you can commit yourself, you will succeed. A path that other people have taken before, and even if they did things slightly differently than you will, they succeeded.

Spoiler alert – if you only give your business a chance you will fail.

Sadly, people give up because it takes too long. It's too hard. It's too much effort.

They start it. They do a little work. They give up because it's not what they were expecting. So you know what? These same people that think it's too much work learning something new and committing to one thing, end up not committing to dozens or hundreds of different things because they always take a chance on them. They do just a little bit to see if it's easy.

It's never easy. But it's always possible.

If you go all in, work the formula for success and you do not give up, you will succeed. It's inevitable.

Fail Faster

One of the key things they teach you at fancy colleges that offer diplomas that unlock amazing opportunities is to fail early and fail often.

The best thing you can do for yourself to fail the right way is to:

- Get comfortable with uncertainty
- Find tools to help you learn from failure
- Learn to turn your failures into opportunities

Failing isn't easy. At first.

There are two types of people can fail and still stay mentally strong.

Idiots don't care if they fail because they make mistakes, don't learn from those mistakes, and then do the exact samething, hoping that something will change.

It won't change. There are plenty of fools out there expecting to do the same thing their entire lives and never change, praying that a miracle will happen, but it never does. Then there are people who have taken the time to deal with their inner demons. That voice inside that that tells you that you're a failure, and a screw-up. These people face their fears and tell their own mind who is boss.

When they experience failure, they see it as an opportunity to learn and grow, not a personal shortcoming.

When they take on new projects, they calculate the value of starting the right way so that any mistakes and failures made along the way are lessons.

When they go into a situation where they're going to fail, they bring tools to help them navigate, bounce back, grow and even thrive in the face of every one of their failures.

Because each failure is good. It's another step closer to massive success.

The secret is that nobody is born this way. The only way to become mentally strong and comfortable with failure through practice and education.

That could be you.

That will be you if you stick with the program I've outlined in this book.

Successful people realize that the faster you fail, the faster you learn. The faster you make mistakes and learn from them, the faster you achieve success.

Learn From Other People's Mistakes

It might seem obvious, but if you can figure out how to learn from other people's mistakes, then you might not have to make those same mistakes yourself. This could save you hours, weeks, or years of wasted time in making your own mistakes, and possibly thousands, tens of thousands, or even millions of dollars which you might not have to throw away on valuable mistakes.

Ideally, you want to get get specific feedback about how mistakes were made and why. You can use this to take action and steer clear of common pitfalls that would cause you to make your own mistakes.

This will allow you to become mentally prepared for success. It doesn't mean you won't ever make mistakes in the future. Of course you will. And every mistake you make will bring you that much closer to success.

Learning from my mistakes will allow you to launch past everyone else, especially if you compare yourself to the person you would be if you hadn't learned anything – the you that would still be struggling and never accomplish anything because they gave up too soon.

When I discovered that I could completely change my life and the lives of others around me by committing to selling products on Amazon using Fulfilment By Amazon, I launched myself into the business one hundred percent.

No looking back, no regrets.

I spent about six months trying to figure the system out, making mistakes that over time, I made my money back from and did better than breaking even, although not enough to really call it a good profit.

I learned what I was doing wrong with those products and finally hit on one item that started bringing me in six figures per year. I don't think I would have found that item or known what to do with it if I didn't fail on those other learning lessons first.

I then continued to spend years of my own time making mistakes. I screwed up. I took some chances because I got cocky about my wins. I launched a few things that looking back on it were pretty dumb, and I didn't launch a few things that other people went on to make millions of dollars on.

I don't feel bad about any of that.

Every mistake I made, I went back to see what I could learn from it.

I learned my lesson. I went on and made different mistakes, but each failure allowed me to develop a system which works for me now. It's a system that has brought me in many new products that sell five, six, and seven figures per year.

I then taught this system to my friends and family, and then started teaching the AMZ Method to thousands of students from over 100 countries around the world – and it worked.

It continues to work because it's based on my own mistakes that cost me millions of dollars and years of my life invested in learning from them. My students don't have to spend those years, or a million dollars making their own mistakes. They can learn from my mistakes, and use the proven method for success.

CHAPTER 4

THE PSYCHOLOGY OF AMAZON CUSTOMERS

"YOUR CUSTOMERS ARE" responsible for your company's reason for existing."

• *Marilyn Suttle*

I'm going to break this chapter down in one easy step.

Experts get all markety and guru-y and intellectual trying to answer this really simple question, but it's much simpler than that.

Why do people buy anything on Amazon?

Don't overthink it – you already know the answer. Do you know why you already know the answer to that question?

Because you've already bought stuff on Amazon. It's likely you've bought tons of stuff before. You probably even have something in your cart right now, and something on the way to be delivered to your house.

You are an Amazon customer. It's likely that you bought things from Amazon for the same reason everyone else in the world does.

Amazon is easy.

You don't have to go to the store, so you save time on driving and parking, you save money on gas. You can shop for almost anything in the world with your newborn baby sitting in your lap, click a button, and a day or two later, they bring it to your house.

Amazon has quality items and you can pick the best from tons of different categories. You can easily compare items.

Amazon has great customer service. If someone wants to return something, no problem they just fill out a return label and ship it back for free.

Amazon has pretty much everything that anyone is looking for in one stop, from full-sized furniture to fill up the house, to cleaning products, to toys for kids, groceries, clothes. It's all there.

Amazon sells products to more than 300 million people around the world.

More than two in every three households in the USA is subscribed to Amazon Prime, which means they get free 2-day delivery on almost everything on the site.

People love Amazon. They trust it. They buy from it again and again.

Here's why.   • • •

Trust

People buy from stores that they trust.

Amazon has proven to be a reliable, trustworthy store. It's easy to use their search engine to find exactly what you need. You can then compare different models of items, often using a side-by-side comparison chart.

All of the item specifications are clearly written into a designated area, and there are clear photos of the item you're looking to buy.

Customers are allowed to review the item, leaving an honest impression of their experience. The reviews are then tallied and you can immediately see the overall score, out of five possible stars. If you're curious, you can scroll down and read every single review, to find out more details.

This is something you can't even get if you walk into a store in person.

If you walk into a knife store and you're surrounded by knives that all look really similar, you really don't know the difference between a $5 dollar knife and a $500 dollar knife. You don't know if the $5 dollar is a great value for the low price, or maybe the $500 dollar knife is a total rip off and you're only paying for the name brand.

On Amazon you can see thousands of reviews for those same two knives and make a trusted decision in under a minute.

Amazon also reliably ships items and takes back anything you need to return, usually for free. A few days after ordering, your item shows up in an Amazon box, undamaged and in good condition. Their lenient return policy allows you to return almost anything, for any reason, by printing out a return label and taking it to the post office, or even shipping it back from your own home.

Once people have a number of really positive experiences with Amazon, they become dedicated customers. Because of consistently good customer service and building trust, people are more likely to use Amazon again and again – especially if they have the need for items, and it's convenient, both of which are also true.

Need

People need stuff. Especially consumable goods.

We will keep buying stuff because it's in our nature to make sure that we are prepared, whether it's by getting food to feed ourselves or our families, camping gear, furniture, cleaning products, exercise gear, books, toys or any number of hundreds of thousands of other things. We always want to have items on hand that we need.

We buy things when we're celebrating and giving gifts, we buy things when we're feeling sad and want to fill that empty void inside of us.

We buy consumable goods and then we buy things we think are permanent, but then they break. So ultimately, everything is a consumable good. We might wish that new phone or tablet are going to last forever, but it's likely they have four or five good years before they also need to be replaced.

Note how I didn't say that people want stuff. They need it. They have to have it. So they buy it.

As you will come to find out, there's also a hidden switch inside the human brain that tells us the difference between a small purchase and a big purchase.

We can make twenty small purchases at $10 apiece in a single day and easily spend $200 to check out in our Amazon cart, but we might be more cautious to make a single $100 big purchase on that same day.

Weird, huh?

Convenience

If you can make someone's life a little easier, you can turn that into a business.

This is the exact model that Amazon follows. Things are easy to find, easy to add to your cart, easy to check out. Shipping is easy and returns are easy. There's nothing complicated about it. It's so simple, even a kid can use it. I know, because my kids use it to order stuff.

Convenience is in big demand because so many other things in life are hard.

Relationships are hard. Willpower is hard. Figuring out how you're supposed to balance your diet and exercise and do all the stuff on your to-do list while still staying sane is hard.

But when you show up to Amazon, everything is easy. No wonder they have so many loyal customers!

Now that you know that people buy on Amazon because of the Trust, Need, and Convenience factor, it's time to investigate the psychology of what people need even deeper. Don't worry, it's not complicated, it's actually still pretty simple.

Law of Supply and Demand

From the beginning of time, throughout the existence of humans, there has been a universal Law of Supply and Demand.

When people need things, that need has to be fulfilled. It does not matter how far we evolve, or even if we have flying cars and cryptocurrency that we use as our standard for cash in the next few years.

People need stuff.

When they go to buy those things, other people need to have that stuff for them.

That's how simple this all is.

It used to be that people needed lumber and stone to build their houses. People needed food to feed themselves and their families.

When they needed those supplies, they had to go collect the lumber, collect the stone, and collect the food themselves.

Pretty soon, smart people realized they could specialize and get really good at collecting something. They could go collect a bunch of lumber and then trade that to other people for food, or the things they needed.

It still works that way.

When you need a broom, you don't go out into the forest and grab a branch and some straw to make your own broom. Those days are over, although the law of Supply and Demand is still around.

You don't even have to leave your house to get a broom. You take your phone out of your pocket, go on Amazon, find a broom, and one minute later you click a single button. Within a day or two, you get that broom delivered to your house.

People buy thousands of brooms every single day. Hundreds of thousands of brooms per year. Brooms get old. They break. People need new brooms.

Someone has to make brooms for those people to buy.

That someone could be you. It's your job to find out what people need and then help them fill that need by making sure there's a product they can buy. Master that one concept and you're going to be a millionaire.

Now that you know that people are guaranteed to be buying things from now until the end of existence, it's time to find out how to get these things and sell them.

CHAPTER 5

PRODUCT PROBLEMS VS. PEOPLE PROBLEMS

"YOU'VE GOT" *to start with the customer experience and work back toward the technology - not the other way around.*

• Steve Jobs

If you point your finger at someone, or something, just know that there are three fingers pointing back at you.

Go ahead, try it. Your index finger is pointed out, but there are still three of your own fingers pointed straight back at you. When you try to place the blame on someone, or something else, just know that you're also responsible.

I say this because most people's first instinct is to blame. That's how I was when I was young, and that's how my kids were born. It's a natural part of being human, to place the responsibility on someone else, or something else.

"Sorry, teacher. He made me hit him because he said something mean to me."

That's not right, is it? Nobody made you hit them by saying something to you. It's still a choice you make.

How To Get Better Products

People ask me all the time when they want to sell stuff on Amazon, how they can get better products.

The answer is easy, but they usually don't like it.

If you want to get better products, then you have to get better.

Don't you point the finger at your product and tell it that it's supposed to do the work for you.

No. You do the hard work in the beginning and create better products. If something goes wrong, it's not your product's fault. It's not Amazon's fault. It's not your friend's or your spouse's or your kid's or anybody's fault.

As a business owner, you have to take accountability. The fault is always yours, and you alone are responsible for your own success.

That's how to get better products, is to get a better you. It's the most honest answer, but it's true, it's real, it's valuable, and you get to become a better person as a side effect.

• • •

How To Get Better

The 1% has what the 99% does not have because the 1% is willing to do what the 99% will not do.

Let that sink in for a moment.

Most of the time, we disregard all the hard work that people do to get where they are. It's so much easier to assume that someone is rich because their parents handed them a ton of money, and sometimes that's true. But there are plenty of instances, myself included, where I was handed nothing but hardships and through my own hard work, made my fortune. If someone saw me out at the mall spending money on my family, it would be easier for them to just assume I was born into money and that's how I earned my fortune, than to admit to themselves that I worked hard for everything I have and that if they worked harder too, they could also have what I have.

The reason that's harder is because it's too real. Now, instead of blaming me for being rich and disregarding my hard work for where I am in life, it's easier for them to make up a story for why I have nice things and they don't.

It's not because I was born rich, it's because I worked for it.

And you could work for it too, if you want it bad enough.

The thing about earning money isn't just having it. I don't like money itself. It doesn't excite me to have a ton of money in the bank, own a number of rental properties and see my sales figures on Amazon. That's not what's important to me.

What I do value is that my money is able to buy me freedom. It can buy me time, which I can use to spend with my family and make an investment I do care about: being a husband and a father.

With more time, I can finally do all the things I wanted to do, but was putting off back when I was busy hustling, working two jobs, volunteering in my spare hours, sleeping only a few hours a day because I was working so hard and not even making any money.

I don't miss those days. But they did make me appreciate even more the time that I now have free. I use my free time and extra money to sit down with my kids and help them with their homework if they ask me for help, get a babysitter to go out on a nice date with my wife, and play football in the backyard with my friends.

I never used to do that stuff, but now I can, because there's a formula for it.

The Free Time Formula

When you have more money, you can get nicer things. But you're still human and you only eat three meals a day, like everyone else. There's nothing much more you can get out of being comfortable and having money that you don't already have access to when you don't have in money.

There's a formula for getting more of the one thing you can buy, which is creating more time to do whatever you feel like doing. You can't literally buy time itself, but you can pay for goods and services that make your life easier, so that you're not doing those things.

More Money = More Freedom = More Time

When I was living in a 400 square foot apartment, I was hustling just to try to make my $375 per month rent. I never had to worry about my lawn, my cleaning lady, or my pool. That was out of the question, so I never expected that to happen for me in my lifetime.

Now, I have a team of gardeners for my property, a pool guy, a cleaning lady and other people on call in case I need help.

I don't enjoy cleaning my pool and I'm not even any good at it. It's worth it for me to pay someone to come clean my pool. It's a very small fraction of my monthly budget, and it frees up a few hours of a job I would not like to do.

I don't want to clean up my dog's poop. We have a guy come in and scoop up the poop to keep our yard clean. It's a job that I don't want to do, and nobody else in my family wants to do it. We hire someone, and it frees up more of our time.

That's one of the biggest benefits of making more money. When I outsource all those jobs I never wanted to do, I can focus on the stuff that matters to me more, like my work and my family.

Your Covenant

• • •

If you put an excuse in front of your desirable outcome, your desirable outcome will never happen.

For example, have you ever decided you were going to go to the gym to get fitter, stronger, and be healthy?

But you never went. You gave up.

You stopped going.

Did you ever become more fit, healthier or stronger after choosing not to start, or by making an excuse?

You want to live a healthier life, but you don't know how you can fit the gym into your schedule.

You want to get stronger, but you don't know if you can afford the membership.

You want to get thinner, but you don't know if you can eat things that you don't like, or eat small portions, or build that discipline.

If there is an excuse in front of a desirable outcome, your desirable outcome will never happen. It is the law.

Your desirable outcome to change your life should be to learn how to, commit to, and then make a lot of money starting an online business that works for you without you working for it. An online business that will earn you revenue every single month.

Your desirable outcome is to have more health, wealth, and happiness. Your desirable outcome is to spend more time doing what you love with whom you love, when you want, and how you please. These are desirable outcomes.

But if you have an excuse in front of that desirable outcome, it will never come true.

Back in the day, people's word used to mean something. If someone said they were going to do something, they did it. When people made commitments, they followed through.

Why?

They made a covenant.

A covenant is an incredibly powerful bond, which is made up of your word. It used to involve the cutting of flesh in Biblical times, but these days it's okay to use a pen and paper– as long as you still take it seriously.

I want you to make a covenant to yourself. I want you to make a commitment that you will not break. The words themselves are simple, and following them will take willpower, but I know you can do it.

I want you to write this down. Not on your phone. I want you to literally write it down and say it out loud. Say it out loud every single day if you need to, until you truly believe it. Until you do it. Until it's a part of you.

I will show up.

I will not make excuses.

I will take action.

I will not give up.

That is your covenant to yourself.

For those of you who are serious and not curious, make this covenant and don't lie to yourself. Don't cheat yourself out of a promise to you, the most important promise you will make, which is to be constantly show up and do what needs doing.

If you're going to take accountability, change yourself and your circumstances by starting an online business so that you can have the wealth to free up your time and live better, then make a covenant to yourself and don't you ever, ever, lie to you.

CHAPTER 6

THE MILLION DOLLAR QUESTION

"IF YOU DON'T FIND *a way to make money while you sleep, you will work until you die".*

• *Warren Buffet*

I'm offering you a million dollars right now, with one question.

To collect on this million dollars (or more) you need to ask yourself this question. You need to come up with a real, honest-to-God answer for this question. And if your answer is yes, then you need to make a commitment to yourself that you're going to do everything in your power to take massive action and make it happen for you.

Do you want to learn a high-income skillset?

That's it.

You either do, or you do not.

If you do not, no problem. I thank you for reading this far. The rest of the book has no value for you, so please go back to your everyday life with my blessing. If it doesn't work out, maybe come back to this book when the pain of not being successful is greater than the fear of trying something new.

God bless. Go home.

If you do want to learn a high-income skillset, open an online business, completely change your life, live comfortably for the rest of your life, and set up a legacy business for the people you leave behind in this world, then please, read on.

Action and Execution

The difference between people who become successful and those who do not are the ones who take action, and the ones who execute.

That's it.

Energy goes where energy flows.

If you can turn yourself into a conduit, that thing that lets electricity flow through it, then you can take in all the possibilities of the world, all the energy, and then release all that energy back out into the world, but even stronger because it's magnified and focused.

If you can learn how to take action and do what you need to do – and you should learn how to do this because you literally just made a covenant where you wrote it down and promised yourself that you were going to do this – then you will separate yourself from most people out there.

Maybe I made it sound like half the people in the world can take action and execute, and half can't. Nope. It's more like 1% of the people I know that can take action and execute. That might sound elite, or impossible, but it isn't. I was part of the 99% of people who didn't do anything but hope my life would change, and hope something great came along.

A great thing came along and I changed, which lifted me out of that 99% and into a new way of being for myself.

It's about so much more than just having an online business, too.

When my wife asks me to do something, I do it. Not just because she asks me, but because I want to. The steps are clear and it's easy for me to take action, do the task, get it done, and then be done with it.

If she asks me to walk the dog I don't sit down and watch one more episode of my favorite TV show, then make a snack, then sort my stamp collection.

I just walk the dog.

It's amazing how simple it is to take action, but how most people don't do it.

I can say, as a former don't-do-it guy, that I can relate to that. I used to make excuses and procrastinate, too. But now everything is easier because I tell myself to do it and I do it. I have a pretty cool boss, because my boss is me.

• • •

How You Do Anything Is How You Do Everything

There is a little more to it than just taking action and executing. You also have to do it well. Not just sometimes, or with some things, but with all things, all the time.

It's all too easy to get lazy, spoiled, entitled, or half-ass something. But where will you draw the line? What will you commit your full effort into and what won't you?

This is why I hire a pool guy to clean my pool. I don't like cleaning my pool. For me, I don't want to commit my time and energy to doing something I don't want to do. So I hire someone to do it for me. That's not half-assing it. That's delegating.

How you show up and do anything in life is how you do everything. If you don't believe it, look around you. Start with yourself and your own actions, then check and see how your friends and family do things.

If someone shows up and does a sloppy job on their

homework, they're going to develop that habit and do a sloppy job at work, and probably have a sloppy house and a sloppy marriage.

If someone cheats on a test, they might cheat on their taxes, or cheat on their partner.

But if someone invests the time and energy to do it right the first time and learn what they're supposed to, they're more likely to show up and be present at work, which will probably get them promoted, and show up and be present for their partner, which will help develop a long and lasting love relationship that's flexible enough to withstand anything because they care enough to be present and listen and learn.

How you do anything is how you do everything.

After helping thousands of people across the globe become financially independent and open up their own profitable businesses, this is the number one metric I can use to measure if someone will become successful or not.

If I see someone using shortcuts early on, not following the formula, or trying to use their opinions they showed up with instead of research – I know they're going to fail in their online business.

When I see someone doing the work, taking accountability, following the formula, and learning from mistakes – I know they're going to succeed in their online business.

I actually found this to be true in fields outside of opening an online business with Amazon, too. People taking shortcuts and trying to find an easier way usually spend their lives working hard because they never succeed at anything.

If you can learn to show up and be present and learn when you start your Amazon business, you're also going to implement this in anything and everything that you do in the rest of your life. This will increase your results, and how effectively you do everything.

It will increase your effectiveness as a human being, and you will very likely be much happier because you're someone who has something to contribute to the world.

In Order To Be Prolific, You Have To Be Specific

• • •

Knowing what you know now, you can go into this million- dollar question with the knowledge that it's possible to change your life, but it's going to take some up-front hard work on your part to build a system, and work the system.

Once the system is built and you've got income flowing into your bank account, you can buy yourself more time, more freedom and kick back a little to relax, if you so choose.

Armed with this information, ask yourself again: Do you want to learn a high-income skillset?

If you do, read through the rest of this book to find out how. It is about you opening your own business online. It is about using the power of Amazon, a retail giant, to help you connect with more people and sell things to them. It is about branding, building a listing, finding the products, finding the supplier, sourcing the products, managing the shipments, building the listing, doing the SEO, doing the keyword research, reaching out to influencers on your behalf, managing your account, running your PPC, handling ship- ment, and more.

It will take a lot of hard work personal growth, but you will be rewarded with a better life.

I don't say that lightly. It's not just about making more money. The people I have helped to build better products, I have first helped to become better people.

I've seen it pay off in their online businesses. I've seen it pay off in their marriages.

How you do anything is how you do everything.

If you're ready to learn an incredibly valuable skill, in terms of making more money and becoming a better human being, then please read on to part two, where I'm going to teach you the exact system for how I made tens of millions of dollars with my own online business.

CHAPTER 7

KNOCKING DOWN THE DOMINOES

"COURAGE IS YOUR NATURAL SETTING. *You do not need to become courageous, but rather peel back the layers of self-protective, limiting beliefs that keep you small"*.

• *Vironika Tugaleva*

It's easy for people to come up with reasons why they can't start a business – not enough time, not enough money, not the right skillset, they're only going to get one shot and if they fail then that's it.

Every single one of those excuses is a self-limiting belief. It's a lie you keep telling yourself because secretly, deep down, you're afraid of change – even if it's good.

Isn't that remarkable?

People don't really want to change, even if it's change for the better.

We're more comfortable in a routine, a pattern, a habit, even if it's negative and brings us pain. It's easier to do nothing and stay where we are, than ever improve.

It's like seeing an elephant tied up with a rope.

You could hold that rope, or tie it to a post and the elephant will assume that it's tied up in captivity.

The elephant, which weighs 8,000 pounds, could tug that rope and break its bonds in a single second. It could drag you with, snap the post, and be free if it chose to.

But the elephant sees only the rope and admits defeat without struggling to break free.

If you see an excuse holding you back from success, you are that elephant.

No time? Make time.

No money? Borrow money.

Not the right skillset? Learn the skillset (it's all in this book!).

You only get one shot? Ridiculous, go back and read about failure and why it's essential to your own personal growth, and your business.

Out of excuses? Great! Let's knock down the dominoes that are holding you back so you can build a successful online business.

Here are the biggest road blocks that I have seen with the thousands of people I've worked with.

• • •

Fear Of Failure

Some fears are natural. If you're standing at the edge of a five-hundred-foot cliff and think to yourself that if you fell off that cliff that you might die, you are correct. This fear is a natural life-saving instinct that usually keeps us from doing stupid things (as long as we're not doing it for the gram, some people die for a good selfie).

Now you're on the edge of a building and you're three stories up. You're naturally afraid of falling over the edge because you could die, or break your limbs.

Now you're on the edge of a railing, and that same fear pops up. You probably won't die if you fell over a railing and hit the ground. You probably wouldn't even break a limb. But it's still scary.

Now you're on the edge of a curb and your mind is racing. That same thought of maybe breaking a limb is para- lyzing you from stepping down only six inches. You would have a very difficult time dying, breaking a limb, or even getting a scraped elbow from this very short height. But something is preventing you from doing it.

Do you see how easy it is to start equating one failure with another?

It's a false analogy. You're not going to get hurt if you step off that curb. You could probably also hop over that railing safely. In an emergency, you would be able to figure out how to safely get down from that three-story building.

But some of us try something and it doesn't work, so we build up a lie inside of our mind that we're not good enough, and we're just going to fail if we try again.

The problem with that is you can't get better if you don't fail. You're supposed to make mistakes and learn from them.

If you took a chance on one cryptocurrency coin and it didn't work out for you, that doesn't mean that cryptocur- rency never makes anyone rich. Actually, it's made more millionaires than anything else on earth.

Your limited experience doesn't make you right, it makes you afraid.

You're reading this book right now because you have a desirable outcome. You do want things to change. You do want to rise up past the fear of failure to become successful.

The fear of failure is natural. Overcoming that fear is difficult.

This is why some people succeed where other people do not. They're willing to face their fear and overcome it so that they can If you're ready to go all in and never give up, then you're already different. If you can follow through with what you set out to do then you will be successful.

Fear Of Market Saturation

Do you remember the Law of Supply and Demand?

Understanding market saturation is a game changer.

People are naturally fearful that there's no room in the market for new things because everything exists.

I heart that.

But why is there a Walgreens literally right next door to a CVS? Why is there a McDonalds in the same shopping plaza as a Wendy's, Burger King, and Taco Bell? Why is there a Lowe's across the street from a Home Depot?

Talk about a saturated market. If I were inside the store, I don't know if I could even tell if I was inside a Lowe's or a Home Depot because they're almost identical. They sell the same thing at almost exactly the same prices, to the same people.

Competition exists all around us.

What do you notice when you walk down the cereal aisle at the grocery store? How many different cereals do you see? Hundreds? A thousand?

Sometimes, there are even twenty different types of the same cereal: Cheerios, Honey Nut Cheerios, Apple Cinnamon Cheerios, Multi-Grain Cheerios, Chocolate Cheerios, Fruity Cheerios, Frosted Cheerios, Cheerios Oat Crunch Almond, Cheerios Oat Crunch Oats N' Honey, Chocolate Peanut Butter Cheerios, Chocolate Strawberry Cheerios, Honey Nut Chee- rios Medley Crunch, Multi-Grain Cheerios with Real Straw- berries, Pumpkin Spice Cheerios, Very Berry Cheerios and Honey Nut Cheerios Treats Bars.

Every one of those products takes up space on the grocery store shelf and sells a ton of product every day.

People are naturally fearful that there's no room in the market for new things because everything exists.

I heart that.

But why is there a Walgreens literally right next door to a CVS? Why is there a McDonalds in the same shopping plaza as a Wendy's, Burger King, and Taco Bell? Why is there a Lowe's across the street from a Home Depot?

Talk about a saturated market. If I were inside the store, I don't know if I could even tell if I was inside a Lowe's or a Home Depot because they're almost identical. They sell the same thing at almost exactly the same prices, to the same people.

Competition exists all around us.

What do you notice when you walk down the cereal aisle at the grocery store? How many different cereals do you see? Hundreds? A thousand?

Sometimes, there are even twenty different types of the same cereal: Cheerios, Honey Nut Cheerios, Apple Cinnamon Cheerios, Multi-Grain Cheerios, Chocolate Cheerios, Fruity Cheerios, Frosted Cheerios, Cheerios Oat Crunch Almond, Cheerios Oat Crunch Oats N' Honey, Chocolate Peanut Butter Cheerios, Chocolate Strawberry Cheerios, Honey Nut Chee- rios Medley Crunch, Multi-Grain Cheerios with Real Straw- berries, Pumpkin Spice Cheerios, Very Berry Cheerios and Honey Nut Cheerios Treats Bars.

Every one of those products takes up space on the grocery store shelf and sells a ton of product every day.

Saturation can only exist when there is more supply than there is demand.

People have a high demand for products because some things are consumable goods, and other things seem like they're long-term purchases but they're actually consumable goods. That brand new car only has ten to fifteen years of life in it, and it's likely the owner is going to change their mind and be in the market for a new car in two to three years.

Saturation exists and it's good to be aware of, but it's not a reason why you can't start a business.

Once you're aware of the concept of saturation, you can actually use it to your advantage to look at the market differently.

Fear Of Idea Theft

A lot of people think that if they're successful selling products on Amazon, that Amazon itself is going to steal their idea.

First of all, if anyone steals your idea, it's theft of intellectual property and you have a profitable lawsuit on your hands.

But more than that, Amazon makes their money in advertising. They make their money in the back end, taking a small chunk of everything that gets sold on their site.

Your success is their success. The more you sell, the more they make. The more you spend money on ads, the more they make. The more you link outside of Amazon and bring in customers to buy your products, the more they make.

That's why they're the biggest business in the entire world.

But that also leaves you plenty of space to open up your own online store and sell a ton of products with their services.

They allow you to access their multi-billion-dollar website, customer service, and Prime Delivery service. They built all that so you could sell more, so no, they're not going to steal your idea.

The reason why Amazon sellers make so much money, and the reason why this online business is so profitable is because Amazon makes it very simple for you the seller to open up a store and sell what you've got.

It costs Amazon zero dollars to sell advertisements, for which they make billions.

Fear of Scams

SCAM stands for 'still confused about money.'

Do you know why people think that something is a scam? Because, they weren't introduced to it, and nobody in their family tree was introduced to it.

But let me tell you what the biggest scam out there is. Were you taught that you have to exchange your time, which is your most valuable asset, for money? You were supposed to go out and get a good education so you could get a good job, then trade the few precious hours of your life away for just enough to get by?

That's a scam.

My entire family came from Puerto Rico. My grandfather died in the hood and lost his house. No one in my family could buy the house that my grandfather lost for $30,000. Nobody had that kind of money.

My grandfather worked his entire life in a steel mill and died in poverty.

I love my family to death, but you can't take marriage advice from your divorced uncle. Therefore, you shouldn't take financial advice from people in your family tree or someone who you know, who is not where you want to be.

If someone who isn't financially successful tells you that something is a scam, then they're still confused about money. And I would also say that older generations don't understand how the internet works. Not just checking your email, but waking up to the fact that we have over 2 billion global buyers in 2021.

The internet isn't just a fad, it's the future of business. If you can get into it now, then you can become part of that future.

Now there may be more than just scams, idea theft, market saturation, or failure holding you back. Perhaps you don't have a clear path on exactly what steps to follow for success in your online business.

I'm going to clear that up in the next chapter.

CHAPTER 8

THE AMZ FORMULA

"I CAN GIVE you a six-word formula for success: think things through - then follow through."
> • *Eddie Rickenbacker*

My success could have been an outlier, just a little blip on a stats sheet where I got lucky and hit the right market at the right time. As I said earlier, success should not have come to me because I came from nothing and had every disadvantage possible, except for one.

I was committed to finding something else to change my life and then following through until I changed it.

That one little mentality shift is everything you need to succeed. That and a clear plan.

I wanted to see if anyone could follow the steps that I followed to enjoy the same kind of success as me.

They did. My friends and family did. People who came to me seeking advice did. They all succeeded.

I started to teach it to people. Lots of people. People around the world. Thousands of people in over 100 countries have learned this method from me and it changed their lives because it worked.

These are all different types of people that it worked for, no matter what your ethnicity or religion is, male and female, many different nationalities.

It worked for the ones who believed in themselves, started out, followed through and followed the formula. If you were waiting for a miracle to happen to help change your life and your circumstances, this is that miracle.

You have to take advantage of the opportunity of a lifetime during the lifetime of the opportunity. That being said, here is the exact formula that I teach people that earns them a passive full-time income, and often brings them incredible wealth beyond what they imagined.

The AMZ Formula

The AMZ formula was named that because it covers the bases, A through Z of everything you need to sell on Amazon, or AMZ.

There are three parts to the AMZ formula. Each one is absolutely essential to the whole. You can't just pick and choose.

There is plenty of room for creativity once you know these rules, but if you don't follow the rules then I can't guarantee your success. In fact, I have seen plenty of people just focus on one of these parts and think they're going to open a successful business, but then they don't because each part is one section of the whole system.

In this chapter I'm going to briefly cover the three major parts of the formula, then get into each of these in more depth in future chapters.

The AMZ Formula is built on understanding and implementing:
1. Risk Tolerance
2. Available Investments
3. Desired Net Profit

It sounds deceptively simple, because there's a lot more to it than just that. But at its core, it's also a very simple system. While learning what these things are and how you can use them is a little tricky, it's a breeze once you get the hang of each element.

Risk Tolerance

• • •

Are you comfortable taking risks?

When you can answer a series of questions, you can find out how comfortable you are at taking risks. This is your Risk Tolerance.

Everything in this life is a gamble, to some extent. You're reading this book right now, assuming you have more life ahead of you, and that an airplane doesn't go wonky and crash into your house. You're taking a risk getting married, having a kid, getting a new job, riding a bike, driving a car.

Everything is a risk because you could die at any second.

But that doesn't stop you from going to the grocery store to get more food because you think you're going to keep living.

That's Risk Tolerance. Yes, there's a chance you could crash your car or someone could crash their car into you, but you still drive.

In business, you basically want to see how comfortable you can get with being uncomfortable. Ask yourself the following questions to see what your Risk Tolerance is.

How long can you wait to get a return on investment?

That's when you make money off the money you put in.

How fast do you need a return? That's when you can pay back any money you borrowed, using the money you made.

How big of a return do you need? You want to make sure it's worth your time to borrow money and then make money on that money.

How long can you wait? You will need to pay back your borrowed money at some point, plus you have bills to pay. You want to know that you're going to make your money back in time to pay it back, if you borrowed it, and so that you can pay your rent, car, and power bill.

How much can you invest? Maybe you already have a little money sitting around, or maybe you have good enough credit, or kind enough family members that you can borrow some money that you're going to make money back on.

These are all questions that you need to ask yourself and answer to the best of your ability. Once you understand your Risk Tolerance, you can move on.

Available Investments

This is how much money you start out with.

It doesn't have to be your money, but you do have to be able to invest it.

Imagine you're going to invest in the stock market because you heard that it pays well. You can either start out with your own money, or borrow money from someone else. If you make money, you can now pay back that person with the money you borrowed, plus interest, and then keep anything else you made as profit. This is risky, because while over time the stock market usually goes up, there's also a chance that you can buy in when it's high and then it dips down and you lose money in the short-term.

Now say you're going to buy a house. Same as the stock market, you borrow money from a bank and buy a house. You hold onto it for ten years and it doubles in value.

Meanwhile, you've been paying off that house loan from the bank a little bit at a time. You're nowhere near paid off on that house, but if you sell it for twice what you paid for it, ten years in the future, you can now take half the money from the sale and pay back the bank, then keep the other half of the house sale as profit.

That's how smart investors make a ton of money on real estate. But it takes a long time.

For your business, you're going to invest your own money, or borrow money from a bank, from friends, or family, then make something. You're going to sell that thing that you make on Amazon and people are going to buy it. There's a whole entire chapter over what you should create later on, but for now, just know that you're going to need a little bit of money to start this online business, just like you would for any other business you start.

Desired Net Profit

Your desired net profit is how much money you want to make on a single item you're going to sell on Amazon.

Let's be real. When we're talking numbers, products can make a few million dollars per month, but that's going to take a much bigger available investment than you probably have. It's going to take a much higher risk tolerance than you prob- ably have.

Dream big, but think smart. Work your way up to the million dollar a month item by making ten items that make ten thousand dollars per month. By then, your risk tolerance will be higher because you're smarter and more capable at sales, plus you should have a lot more money to work with and so more available investment.

When you can become specific about what your risk toler- ance is, what your available investment is, and how much you want to make per product, then you've completed the first part of the AMZ formula. Thus will allow you to much more easily find what product you're going to create and sell. A good starting range for a very successful product should be around $3,000 to $10,000 profit per month. That's between $36,000 to $120,000 per year, if you multiply that by 12 months.

Not bad for one product you can leave on autopilot and sell for the next 20 or 30 years. But some of you are replacing very highly paid jobs where you're already making over $100,000 and $200,000 per year.

All you need are more products. You can always scale your business bigger and better and there are chapters on that later in the book, but for now you just need to figure out what your desirable outcome is.

Patience, Persistence, and Resilience

The three pillars of success, are Patience, Persistence, and Resilience.

I literally wear this on my wrist every single day – not because I'm superstitious, but because I know how much hard work and focus it takes to become successful.

If you can follow the above formula and be patient, be persistent, and stay resilient, then you will absolutely succeed.

People fail in this business because they get impatient, it's not performing fast enough. They fail because they give up on themselves and their business when they would have done just fine if they stuck it out. They fail because there's one small problem and they can't let go of it. They get one bad review and quit.

Go check out how many one-star reviews there are for the Harry Potter and you will see that resilience is essential to any business. While some sad nobody was leaving J.K. Rowling another 1-star review on her book, she was busy writing the next book in a billion-dollar franchise.

Still Stuck?

Call us at +(512)-548-2467 and we can tell you what the next best move is. We offer a host of services designed to un-stuck you and kickstart your business, or get you to the next level.

CHAPTER 9

YOU'RE ONLY ONE PRODUCT AWAY

"I NEVER DREAMED ABOUT SUCCESS. *I worked for it.*"

• *Estée Lauder*

A long time ago, there were two miners working a mine shaft that they shared. They knew the area was rich in gold because they had found some pretty decent sized nuggets. It was enough to pay for their lifestyle, food and gear.

Day after day, they uncovered enough gold to get by. But a few months in, one of the miners quit. He handed over the mine shaft to his friend, along with his mining tools. Then he moved back to Virginia where he went back to shoveling horse manure. He died a few years later from disease.

The other miner kept at it. The first day he was alone in the mine, he made a commitment that he wouldn't give up because he wouldn't go back to shoveling horse manure. He mined his hardest, and by the end of the day, he struck a vein of gold so rich that it only took him a few more days to mine enough to set himself up for life. Within a few weeks, he was wealthier than he had ever been in his wildest dreams.

He wrote to his friend, but the letter never made it. So he enjoyed his rich lifestyle in a new land where he could finally afford to buy a house, get married and have a dozen kids.

Now, this parable may not describe your situation, but often times we don't know how close we are to striking gold when we quit. Some people run 25 miles of a marathon and give up, so they run 25 miles back to the start.

No matter where you are on your path to success, you're where you need to be to learn, grow, and get better at what you do. If you follow the AMZ Formula and stick to the intelligent blueprint laid out in this book, it's a recipe for success as long as you stick with it.

I'm not saying that you're going to strike gold your first time out, but I've developed a fool-proof system for recouping your losses so you can try again with another product if your first one is a lesson in what you can improve.

Remember the AMZ Formula may be fool-proof, but it's not quitter-proof. You're only one product away from striking gold – you just don't know which product that will be.

Here are some more interesting ways that you can find that one product that can bring you in a year's salary without doing any work, or even set you up for life.

• • •

Five Ways Not To Launch A Product On Amazon

You should expect to put in some work on the front end to create an item that people are going to buy. This doesn't mean you have to invent new stuff that nobody has never heard of (bad idea). It means being clever about what you create and make a version of that doesn't already exist.

Basically, don't be lazy and copycat other items.

I'm going to start with what doesn't work, because although it may seem obvious, it's the first thing that newcomers think to try. While it's okay to have a saturated market and compete for people's money with a similar product, it's not a good idea to make a cereal called Cheerioz that looks the same, tastes the same, comes in the same package and costs the same amount of money as regular Cheerios.

There are ways to compete that won't get you in trouble and will allow you to actually add value to the market place. You will learn those soon.

For now, pay attention to the following strategies, which don't work well for creating a new product to sell on Amazon. I will add in some easy fixes, as well.

1. Same Design

• • •

If you're offering something with exactly the same design, people will see that in the photos and description of your item.

Easy Fix: change the design.

2 Same Price

If you're offering something with the exact same price as your competition, why? There is plenty of opportunity for a price point structure to make your product stand out. And stick with me, making your item cheaper isn't going to bring in more sales and make you more money – it's usually a race to the bottom that you won't win.

Easy Fix: find out how to offer more value and raise the price.

3. Same Bonuses or Accessories

If you're offering something with the exact same bonuses and accessories as your competition, why? Get clever. What else can you offer as a bonus or accessory that someone else forgot?

Easy Fix: go review mining and check out the reviews for your competition. The 1-, 2- and 3-star reviews often offer specific things that people wanted and didn't get. Give it to them and you've got a winner!

4. Same Packaging

If you're offering something with very similar, or the exact same packaging, why?

Easy Fix: spend a little more to get different packaging. Packaging is a really, really big deal. It's what lets companies like Apple charge 10 x what their competition is charging and get away with it. Their packaging is so well-designed, you know that the computers and electronics inside of them are, too.

5. Same Supplier

If you're offering something that comes from the same supplier and it's actually the exact same thing, this is a big mistake. People know when they're getting the same exact item and they do not like to be fooled.

Easy Fix: find a new supplier to make your item. This is covered in later chapters.

Five Ways to Find A Winning Product On Amazon
• • •

You've seen what not to do, so now, here's more of what not to do. Actually, it's very important to know what not to offer so that you can find out what you should be offering.

Read through this list very carefully and take notes, because note takers are money makers!

Don't break the rules yet. There's a reason I've included these winning strategies in my formula.

I spent thousands of dollars chasing these products with little to no success. I didn't give up, but I did learn from many, many expensive lessons and I've come to realize these things are not worth your time.

Make sure your product is:

1. Not Seasonal

This is a huge mistake that new people make. They want to come in and clean up at Christmas, Halloween, etc. but then they're sitting on a ton of inventory for the other 11 months of the year, paying interest on money they borrowed to create these products. Do not go seasonal, or you may be stuck with stuff you can't sell until the following year.

• • •

2. Not Trending

You want to make sure that you get yourself an evergreen product, which is something that people will always need, like silverware. Even if we have flying cars in the next few years, we will still need to eat with silverware. I spent a ton of money making thousands of fidget spinners. By the time I launched the product, the fad as over and I had to sell them at rock-bottom prices just to get rid of all the product.

3. No Intellectual Property

Amazon's Terms of Service very clearly state that you are not allowed to use intellectual property if it's not yours. Read through that long Terms of Service agreement so you understand it better. No Star Wars, no Legos, no Jimi Hendrix gear. If you don't own the IP, then don't use it.

4. Net Profit 30%+

You need some wiggle room to make sure that you're making money, and that you can cover the average cost of your sales (I'll explain that at the end of this chapter). You want to make sure you're making at least 30% off your items because it will bring you in more proft at the end of the day, and allow for some learning from mistakes in case things go wrong.

. . .

5. Sells Enough Per Month to Generate Desired Profit

You won't really know how much you're going to sell until you launch a product, so this may appear at first to be impos- sible. But you can gauge how much the competition is selling. You want to find something that's affordable enough to get into with the investment money you have, plus something in that sweet spot of bringing in $3,000 - $10,000 per month.

Where To Look For Profitable Products

There's riches in the niches. Look for products that sell pretty well, but that doesn't have a lot of competition.

Tons of people are going to make yoga mats because they're cheap, easy to make, store well, sell well and there's a high demand. There's also high competition. Maybe everyone reads this book and thinks I'm telling them to sell yoga mats. Just do your research first.

Try to find items in niche categories such as:

Over Sized

Some items are considered over-sized, like furniture. They may not qualify for Prime shipping, or cost you a ton of money to ship. I have a friend who makes over $100 million dollars per year selling furniture on Amazon. There is plenty of room for other styles of furniture if you're willing to do the hard work and look.

Over Weight

Some items are considered over-weight, like kettlebells and fitness gear. It also may not qualify for Prime shipping, or cost you a ton of money to ship. But fitness is a huge seller, and there may be a lot of business to be found in busy fitness enthusiasts who want stuff delivered, even if it's not by the next day. Search this category for new products you can create.

1. Semi-Seasonal Products (like pool toys and swimsuits

I know I said no seasonal products, but some things are semi- seasonal. A summer swimsuit might only sell to people in Minnesota for two months out of the year, but you've still got a plenty big audience in California who are going to the beach in December, so you can still sell it throughout the year.

Competitor Stores

You will learn that other people like you have their own stores. You can actually click on those stores to find out what they're selling. Often, sellers find something profitable and offer multiple products because they continue to make good money in that niche. This is a free education for people who click around to see how other sellers have positioned them-selves in the market.

1. Supplier Recommendations

You can find out who is supplying your competitors with their products and politely ask their supplier if they have any recommendations for what's really hot. They know what sells a lot because they actually make it.

There's also some software designed especially for Amazon sellers, which can help you find the right keywords and the right products. You can find out more at:

https://www.amzhunter.com You can even use a special promo code to get 50% off if you decide to purchase, using this when you check out: HUNTER50 AMZ

ACoS

I will try to keep all the math in this book very simple. It's important to know what you're getting into so you can see how much you could earn, so you need to know your ACoS.

ACoS percentage stands for Average Cost of Sale. That's what your product

Amazon will give you a percentage of the entire sale, any time you sell a product. They will also take a percentage for themselves, to store and ship your item all around the world.

So this is very simple.

If your profit margin is 30%, that means you will get 30% of the money your product sells for.

If your ACoS, or average cost of sale is 15%, then you subtract this from your profit margin, and it equals your net profit margin. That's the amount of money that you get to keep.

For example, you're selling a yoga mat for $50. 30% of this is $15, and that's your profit margin. Your ACoS is 15%, which is $7.50.

You take the profit margin of $15 and subtract the ACoS

of $7.50 and you're left with $7.50.

That means that you get to keep $7.50 for every one of those yoga mats that you sell. It might not sound like a lot of money, but you only need to sell 1,333 of those yoga mats per month and you're making $10,000 profit per month. For perspective, that's only 111 yoga mats per day.

Some products will sell more than that many per day, and some will sell less. Some will also bring you in more profit, and some less.

Still Stuck?

Give us a call at +(512)-548-2467 and we can help you figure out what your product is. Don't forget to mention that you

found out about us from this book right here, so we know how best to help you.

CHAPTER 10

FIND THE VALUE OF YOUR PRODUCT

"QUALITY IN A PRODUCT or service is not what the supplier puts in. It is what the customer gets out and is willing to pay for. A product is not quality because it is hard to make and costs a lot of money, as manufacturers typically believe."

• Peter Drucker

In order to get results other people are not getting, you have to do what others are not doing.

Did you notice something in common for all of those no-no rookie movies for coming up with a new product, in the last chapter? People who copycat and make the same thing, that costs the same, looks the same, is the same, are destined to make an expensive mistake.

When it comes to what people want to buy, we always think that we make logical decisions, but in truth most purchasing is impulsive. I've sat down with my sister when she's shopping on Amazon, and she will pay $10 more for the exact same item to make sure it qualifies for $3 free shipping.

That goes for most Amazon customers. They think they want the best price, but actually they want the best value. They don't want the hassle of returning something. They want something they believe will last.

Apple sells their computers for 10 x what their competitors sell for. They don't last 10 x as long, or work 10 x faster, or 10 x better. They just look really cool, have great packaging, they solved a few problems around computers like making them easier to use, and they created an entire brand of cool around their products, where the consumer sees young hip people dancing to their new iPod with AirPods while working in a coffee café.

Nobody buys an apple computer because it's the best price, but they do buy it because they think they're going to get the best value. They pay more for a usable, reliable product that they love.

That's the secret sauce. Value.

If you can find the value of your product and show your shopper what they're going to get for their money, then you're on the way to big sales.

Price Point Structure
• • •

You don't need to invent a products to sell something on Amazon. In fact, that's a bad idea. You want to find a product that's already selling well but could use some friendly competition. I can't stress this enough, you aren't inventing new products, but you also aren't copy-catting products that exist.

You're going to open an online business selling products that are already on Amazon.

Many people find a product that's making money, and they go and do their research, and when it comes time to develop the product, they launch the exact same-looking product. Same size, same shape, same color, same function, same exact design.

Lazy.

One of the easiest ways that you can develop a product and differentiate a product is by changing the design, the size, shape, color, function. Any of it. All of it!

A lot of people launch their business and launch these products, then try to sell the product for the same exact price point.

Why would you do that?

You know why people do this?

The reason why so many people choose the same price point is because they have this mythology. They think if they did the research and see this is a winning product and go to Amazon and see people who are selling the product at this price point, then this must work.

Does that make sense?

Yes, in a way. Success leaves clues. But, guess what?

The key to launching a product that will compete with the best and outlast the rest is focusing on all of these little details, like price point structure. If you've done all the other little details like create a good product that clearly has a demand, and offered up some new things that people want, like better or different sizes, shapes, colors, functions, offerings, designs, even the packaging, then you can increase your price as well.

It should still be a reasonably priced item somewhere in the $20 - $50 range. That's because this allows you to mark your item up enough to keep it profitable, but your customers still consider it a small purchase.

Anything near $100 is a large purchase, and your customer might get shy about ordering something like that. They might think they don't have the money, even if they order $200 in their cart on that exact same day, of smaller items.

Race To The Bottom

I've said this before, but it bears repeating that simply copycatting someone else's idea and charging less money will not get you a nice, profitable item.

First off, it's a risky move. If you're not getting a 30% profit margin then you might not end up with enough money to cover your Average Cost of Sales. Why would you want to open a business where you sold just enough product to break even, or worse – lose money with every sale.

Another reason you want higher than a 30% profit margin is if the product you sell doesn't perform well. If it's selling too slowly and you want to unload, then you can reduce the price to break even, get your money back, and invest in a new product.

But if you already came in with a lowball move and tried to underbid your price, you won't be able to do that.

Trying to sell for the lowest price will be a race to the bottom, because your competitors will simply decrease their prices to match yours. Now neither of you will be making money, but they might have a few million dollars to sit on, to wait out your failure and watch you leave with your tail between your legs.

It's not worth it to go low. Instead, try to think of what value you can add to raise your price and still offer an amazing product for what your customer is paying.

Why Buy It?

Why is your customer going to buy your product? In future chapters, we're going to discuss your listing and what elements will draw in your audience and sell them on your product.

But at its most basic elemental level, people are going to buy your product because it satisfies a need. If you can show someone that you're there to satisfy that need, then you've got a sale.

You have to genuinely care about your product and put in a little bit of extra work to make sure you're satisfying their need, but that extra work required on your part is a good thing. There are plenty of people out there looking to make a quick dollar and copycatting products. If you want to be different, you have to be different.

If you want to get results that other sellers aren't getting, you have to do things they're not doing.

So say someone needs a yoga mat for their yoga class. They get on Amazon and they can get that mat delivered the next day from 10,000 different sellers.

Do they choose the best price?

There's a nice neon yellow yoga mat for $9.99.

No, they don't pick that one. A low price is actually a red flag. It's a sign that the mat is cheap and will easily break. Plus, nobody wants a neon yellow yoga mat.

They see a nice, beautiful name brand yoga mat for $99.99 but that's a big purchase. That's too much money.

Then they see a beautiful yoga mat that offers a non-slip surface. It comes with a free tote bag. It's got a little strap to keep the mat rolled up when you're not using it. It's got a special textured surface to allow the user to balance better.

Plus, it's only $49.99. It's not too big of a purchase, but it's also not cheap. It's the best value.

Guess what? You just sold another yoga mat.

I only use this example because it's practical, and perfectly captures the mentality of most customers. They want to search for a yoga mat on Amazon, scroll the page for 10 seconds, click on the one that looks like it has the best value, then Buy Now.

They want to protect their valuable time, which is why they're buying on Amazon. If you can sell them that experience in under a minute, convincing them that your product is the best value, then you will rack up big numbers in sales.

CHAPTER 11

COMPETE WITH THE BEST AND OUTLAST THE REST

"IF YOU ARE NOT willing to learn, no one can help you. If you are determined to learn, no one can stop you."

• *Zig Ziglar*

A long time ago, there was a slow tortoise, and fast rabbit.

The rabbit was mean, always bullying and heckling the tortoise about how slow he was. It was non-stop insults, for no reason.

So the tortoise asked the rabbit to race him.

The rabbit started cracking up. He knew he was faster. He could literally run circles around the tortoise. He agreed to the race because he wanted to rub it in, to show everyone who was the fastest in the forest. He agreed to the race.

From the get-go, the rabbit hopped along, putting a huge distance between himself and the tortoise. He ran back just to check that the tortoise was still alive. He ran toward the finish line, laughing at how slow the tortoise was.

Beating the tortoise was too easy. He was going to thoroughly embarrass him. So he decided to get close to the finish line and take a nap, so the tortoise could watch him cross the finish line.

But the tortoise was slow and steady. He just kept walking, putting one foot in front of the other.

When he came up to the finish line, there was the rabbit, sleeping on the side of the road. The tortoise passed the rabbit and won the race while the rabbit was sleeping.

Long story short, it's better to be slow and steady, and continue to improve, than to be quick and careless.

A lot of people are impatient and start their business fast. They want fast results and they do things sloppily trying to outpace the competition and beat people to market. In the beginning everything's good, but then they get anxious. They get careless. They get sloppy.

This is a marathon, not a sprint.

This is a business that once it's up and running, will continue to grow. Your online business is just as real as any other real business. You should treat it with the same respect.

Fun fact: Amazon businesses that are built this way, private label product businesses, physical label product businesses, sell for about 12 x the revenue generated. If you build a $1 million dollar business, you can sell it for $12 million, and there are investors lining up, ready to cut you a check.

How to Compete With The Best to Last the Longest

There are four things you can do to win the slow and steady race. These are things that aren't trending, so if you nail them on the first try, you can set yourself up for a product that will sell for the next 20 - 30 years.

Creating something that has a huge value for your customer makes you a memorable brand. If your customer loves what they bought from you and needs to buy it again, then Amazon literally offers them a chance to "Buy It Again" when they do a search for that item again.

If your yoga mat lasted for five years, and they go to buy another one five years later, they're likely to buy from you again if they felt like they got a good value. A $50 yoga mat that lasts five years isn't bad at all, that's $10 per year before it fell apart. They might even be proud that they managed to destroy your high-quality mat with all that yoga they were doing.

How can you implement the following five qualities into every single one of your products so that it creates massive value for your customer, every time?

1. Quality

Focus on being superior. Focus on your product being the best that it can possibly be, because if you're able to provide the best product in the market, your customer won't keep searching, trying to find a new one. If you're constantly focusing on quality, you will not have any issue with people using your item to satisfy their needs.

2. User Experience

How does your customer feel about buying your product? At Chick-fil-A, the food is just okay, but the service is unmatched. That's why people go. They are always seeking a consistent, reliable and positive user experience. How can you be the Chick-fil-A in your industry, even if you make yoga mats?

3. Customer Service

• • •

Many companies on Amazon do not have any customer service whatsoever, other than the standard Amazon return policy. If you add customer service to your products, you will crush your competition. You can add it inexpensively, by hiring a virtual assistant. We always do this for our products, and this one easy thing separates ourselves from the competi- tion. People love to know that they will have the peace of mind to reach someone in case something goes wrong with their product.

4. Maintain Demand

If something's no longer in demand, it's not going to sell. That's simple, right? Yet so many people don't focus on demand and maintaining demand. You can always nurture your customers and find new ways of marketing products that you're already made. You don't have to keep making new items if you have something that's still selling. Maybe there's not currently huge demand for your product that was selling well, but if you keep it around, demand ebbs and flows and you will already have something that people want when it's in demand again.

1. Constantly Improve and Adapt.

Do evaluations quarterly on your products to see how you can improve them. Why? Because no one else does it. And if you want results that others don't get, you must do what others don't do. People think they should just leave the same pictures, same copy, same price, same bonus, same every- thing, then they wonder why new people come in and crush them, and take their market share. People like you, smart investors, can crush them because of this stuff right here.

The Best Is Never Cheap And the Cheapest Is Never the Best.

How much a product costs is not important.

Is it cheap? It's far from cheap, but the best is never cheap. People already know to watch out for cheap, because it also means it will break easily and be a hassle to return. People want the best.

You deserve the best outcome. Your families deserve the best.

Your desirable outcomes from selling on Amazon are higher than what your job will ever produce.

So how do you beat the best? You have these huge brands, huge companies all over Amazon. And you're the smallest person. You're just this little beginner.

How do you beat them? Unorthodox methods, doing the opposite.

In the Bible, there is a shepherd boy by the name of David.

David beat this giant Goliath. Goliath had armor that the Palestines gave him and a big sword. And David had a little piece of leather and a rock that was at his toes, but he beat Goliath.

How?

Focus.

He found where Goliath's armor separated. He practiced. He aimed carefully. He launched a single stone and killed Goliath, not because he was bigger, not because he had better equipment, not because of magic.

David crushed his competition because he had no excuses,

used his resources well, went for it, found the sweet spot and struck when he needed to.

That's it.

WWAD

WWAD stands for What Would Apple Do?

I've mentioned Apple before, because they're an inspiring company.

Their motto is "Think Different."

My motto is "What Would Apple Do?"

They offer computers, tablets, headphones and iPods that are more expensive than any of their competitors. They work well, they look cool, they have a Genius Bar that you can take your product into if you want to learn how to use it, or fix it for free.

Excellent customer service.

They position themselves as the choice of creative people. Same computer as the next guy but it looks cooler, it's easier to use, so you can work your fancy design job in style.

Excellent marketing.

Apple is the most expensive product in its class. It's also the highest consumer purchased electronics brand in the United States, at a higher price point than all of their competitors.

I learned this from Apple: do not compete with price. Price is important, but do not compete in price.

Offer a better product. A cooler product. More convenience. Great customer service. Bonuses. Accessories.

Steve Jobs was an innovator. The company is different. The price point is different. The quality is different. The pack- aging is different. The customer experience is different.

What's something that already exists, that you can change just a little bit? What can you make cooler? What can you add to the customer experience, so you can add to your price? That's what you want to do – not copycat apple, but to think different.

Next Step

You can start taking action right now on what you've learned.

By now, you should already have a pen and paper out and be taking notes on everything in this book.

Make a list for yourself and call it "Think Different."

Write down the numbers one through five, which will be the same as what we learned in the steps above. For what you're considering making and selling on Amazon, write down how you could change an already existing idea for the following:

1. Quality
2. User Experience
3. Customer Service
4. Demand
5. Improvements

What can you add to your product?

Could you make a yoga mat out of bamboo? Can you add slip-grips to that yoga mat?

What problems can you solve for your customer?

Could you hire a virtual assistant to make sure your brand stands out with better customer service?

Could you create a Facebook community of people who need yoga mats?

What can you do to improve the product and the experience?

Get creative, try to get into a flow, and just think of anything that comes to mind, then write it down. You're only one product away, and this might be your one.

Maybe.

Make sure you follow the AMZ Formula and answer these questions first. And please, don't just make a slip-grip bamboo yoga mat because you read it here.

If you're still feeling stuck on finding your product value, give us a call at +(512)-548-2467 . Don't forget to mention that you found out about us from this book right here, so we can hook you up with the right service for you.

CHAPTER 12

IS THAT THE BEST YOU CAN DO?

"I'VE LEARNED *that people will forget what you said, people will forget what you did, but people will never forget how you made them feel."*

• *Maya Angelou*

I'm proud of my accomplishments, making crazy money and teaching people to follow in my footsteps to change their lives and make a real living, to make a life for themselves.

But more than that, I'm proud of how I treat my employees. I run a number of products on Amazon, I have in-person assistants, virtual assistants, I have co-workers who help me to teach others, who help me to market, analyze and advertise on Amazon and Facebook

I have supply chain distributors who make the real things that I make money on.

I'm proud that I treat these people well. All of them.

Finding out how to make money is great, but it won't change how you act just because you have more money. If you give a jerk a million dollars, you have a million-dollar jerk.

If you can become an ethical, kind person who treats others well and genuinely cares about creating products that work for your customers, then you are in the right business. The secret is that you don't have to be nice to get rich, but you will respect yourself more and buy yourself deep and true satisfaction with what you do if you make other people's lives better.

Your Job Is To Humanize the Supply Chain

I didn't quit working at my factory job at the recycling plant to get rich and treat other factory workers like they're garbage. If there's one thing I learned in my life, it's that you should never underestimate a person, because you never know what they're capable of.

The person you're negotiating with might one day take over their company. One of the workers in their factory could easily realize their own value and build their own empire.

People will always remember how you made them feel, even if they don't specifically remember what you do.

Even more than that, treating people with respect and courtesy is always the right thing to do, no matter how anyone else around you is doing business.

Most of the products that I sell on Amazon are made in foreign countries. It's just the way business is done in the world these days, regardless of what your opinion is on foreign policy and trade. It's very difficult and expensive to produce anything in the USA, although I encourage you to look around and try to find the best supplier for what you're making.

Many of the people I work with are in China. They have a huge time difference between my house in Texas, a language barrier because I write to them in English, plus they have different holidays, weekends, and attitudes.

If I send out an email and the person on the other end doesn't respond right away, I do not take it personally. Maybe they're busy doing their job and creating stuff. Maybe they need a translator to see what I'm asking them.

I don't know. Neither do you. So don't take it personally. Instead, be kind, be polite, and ask for reasonable things.

If they make you an offer to create your product and you haggle too hard, you won't get as good of a product. Yes, in some cultures it's either polite or expected to do some negotiation, but if you cut down too hard on the cost of your product, your end result will not be as good.

Maybe they use a different wood, glue, nails, etc. If they need to cut down on the quality of your item because you asked for too low of a price, then your customers are not going to have a good experience, and your product is dead.

• • •

Ask And Ye Shall Receive
("Is that the best you can do?) ask this one question to get a better price
The Bible says, "Ask and ye shall receive."

There's one sentence that I say that has saved me hundreds of thousands of dollars over the years. I can't even think about how much money I've saved with this one sentence.

Are you ready for it?

"Is that the best that you can do?"

That's a ninja hack that's polite, respectful, and allows

the person you're negotiating with to offer you the best price that they can, without feeling belittled.

This line works outside of starting an online Amazon business as well. If someone's coming to paint your house and offers you a quote, you can ask, "Is that the best that you can do?"

If you're trading in your car at the dealership, you can ask, "Is that the best that you can do?"

You would be surprised how this one sentence magically saves you money.

There are also other respectful tactics you can use with your distributor.

Ask for quantity breaks.

If you can order in higher quantity, they can usually save you money without compromising the quality of your product.

• • •

If You Knew Better, You Would Do Better

The biggest expense in life is what you do not know. If you knew how to do these things better, your business would do better. But at the beginning of starting your business, you don't have the wisdom to know better.

Check in with your suppliers and connections. Ask them how they are. Treat people how you want to be treated.

When you're reaching out to anyone for business, your suppliers included, find out stuff about them. Ask them how their day is going.

They're not robots. Ask them a little bit about themselves and it's likely they will do the same and ask about yours. Before you know it, you have a new friend.

You may find out more about that person, that company, or that culture that you didn't know before. And if you have a friend at the company that's supplying you, you will get better service, and better products. That's not why you make friends with people, but it's a nice perk for being a good person.

Negotiate But Never Badger
• • •

When I was new to the business, my supplier told me, "We want to make you happy, you are a good client of ours. But I need you to understand that if we make the product for the price that you want, it is not coming out of our company's margin."

"What you mean it ain't coming out the company's margin?" I asked. "Where's it coming from? I ain't paying for it."

"You are paying for it because you get what you pay for," they replied.

Understand that these companies have to earn a living.

Understand that these companies only make so much money. So while you're battling them for 0.05 cents, trying to save $500 in your order, somebody like me is coming there and asking for the head of their engineering and product development and trying to spend $5 more per item.

When we go to battle and your product breaks, and you get slaughtered with one-star reviews, and mine gets flooded with five-star reviews, with people saying, "It's the greatest product I've ever bought."

You go out of business, I steal your market share. Do not focus on price, you will lose that battle.

The worst thing that you can ever do is to try to make money on the purchasing of your products.

In real estate, you make money on the purchase of the property and you make money from renting it. Because when you exit, you're going to sell it for more than what you bought it for.

That's not what you want to do with these products. You want to spend more money on the front end to develop the best product that's humanly possible, so that you dominate the competition and add more value to the marketplace.

You do not want to try to save a nickel, a dime, or a quarter on the front end and then lose the integrity your product – and yourself in the process.

The 3 Sample/Quote Myth . Busted!

The common advice I've heard is that you always need to get three quotes and three samples from suppliers before you choose one.

There are thousands of suppliers out there that make a living creating products for people. It's what they do. Why would you waste a few hundred dollars and weeks of your time asking for these samples and quotes?

Just go to one supplier, the best one, and don't ask what everybody else has to offer. Ask them if that's the best they can do. See what their timeline is.

If you rush this step and choose the fastest company, then you're cheating yourself. Maybe they're the fastest because they're not made well, or they don't have a long list of clients because they're not that good.

Faster isn't always better. If you want speed, skip the quotes and samples. Hit up the best company and offer them a good price so they can make you a great product.

At Crisp Learning Technologies, the company that I started to help teach people about business, one of my core competencies that I teach is to operate at every level of your business and in your life in excellence.

If you are not operating in excellence, you are compromising.

And nobody wants to deal with your compromise, not your customers, and not your suppliers.

CHAPTER 13

THE MONEY IS IN THE LIST(ING)

"EVERYTHING MUST BE MADE as simple as possible. But not simpler."

• *Albert Einstein*

A young woman signs up for a yoga class.

She realizes she needs a yoga mat. In that instant of her having that thought, she unlocks her phone, clicks on Amazon, uses voice to text to search for a yoga mat, and in less than fifteen seconds, 250,000 yoga mats pop up in her search results.

She's going to buy one of these mats. She needs it. She only wants to spend about a minute or two choosing the best mat. She's on her lunch break and she wants to get back to her grilled salmon Caesar salad. She scrolls down the list of yoga mats.

Your mat is one of those 250,000.

How on earth is she going to choose your mat?

She looks at the pictures and the names of the mats first. "XOBLOX YOGA MAT" is out of the running. The name is too weird.

There's a neon yellow mat that's a hard pass.

"Balance From GoYoga All-Purpose 1/2-Inch Extra Thick High Density Anti-Tear Exercise Yoga Mat with Carrying Strap" has a pretty cool picture of a nicely rolled up yoga mat with a handle and straps. It's in a deep blue. It has 75,000 ratings, and it's only $25.54.

Click. She bought it. It took her less than a minute to have the idea, open the phone, find the item and buy it.

You just made another sale.

In order to get results that others aren't getting, you have to do the things that other people aren't doing. These are those exact steps for how to make a great Amazon listing, which is where the money is.

Why People Buy On Amazon

We've already been over why people buy on Amazon, generally. It's fast, convenient, and inexpensive. But here are four specific things that will help you sell your products on Amazon.

Yes, people go on Amazon because they trust it, but they may have also had bad experiences and gotten cheap things they needed to return, that were a hassle, that left them with a bad taste in their mouth.

People are pretty clever, for the most part. If they see something that they like, they click it and buy it. If they see that something is off, anything, even one tiny little detail, they will skip it and move onto the next thing because there are thousands of other options.

These four elements will make or break sales for your item on Amazon.

1. Picture
2. Title
3. Reviews
4. Price

Picture – A single, very clear photo that takes up at least 80% of the usable space is essential for your primary photo. Then, use all of the available picture slots to show multiple angles and uses for your item. Imagine it as a thumbnail on a phone, because the majority of your buyers are going to see that.

Title – You need a clear title for your item that should describe it exactly, without exaggerating or stuffing keywords into it. It should be legible, easy to read, sound like a real product that someone would want to buy. It should not include your brand name (unless you have a really cool sounding or recognizable brand name).

Bad Example: KWEEWEE YOGA MAT, Yoga mat, large yoga mat, small yoga mat, yoga mat for kids, all colors yoga mat, all sizes yoga mat, best selling yoga mat.

Good example: New and improved large yoga mat, can be used for all things, comes in different sizes.

Reviews - Reviews are very simple – they offer social proof that other people like (or dislike) your item. No one wants to be the first person to buy your item if it has no reviews. Nobody wants to buy anything that no one else likes.

We'll get into that a little bit later. Number four is price points. Very simple. Do your due diligence. Remember, WWAD. Don't be the cheapest, but no, don't go and try to be Hermès. Nobody knows you yet. You don't have the notoriety.

Price – Your price should reflect your value. If you're offering higher quality, better benefits, better design, or all of those things (like you should be) then you can charge a little bit more. For an item where the average price is $50, you can charge a little more. You can get up to $65 or $70 if your item has a better value and offers something unique, and better than the rest. But don't jump up to $350 because you will price yourself out of the market (plus anything over $100 is major purchase in most people's minds. One personal rule for myself that I recommend to my clients, is never end in 9. For some reason it just seems to sell better when I end in random numbers like 29.57, 35.85, 42.34, or 28.72.

Edit Your Listing

It's free to edit your listing.

It takes between an hour and a couple days for the listing to update. But it costs you nothing. I know so many people who just list their item on Amazon, set it and forget it.

This is possible, but why?

If it's a free, easy tool that can help you get more sales and convince more people that your item is the one to buy, then why not make it as good as can possibly be? Why not study the market every few months and make your listing even better – even more relevant to right now?

If you don't do that, someone else will see that you're selling well. They will sneak in, and they will take away your sales because they're going to make a great listing.

Make sure your listing is excellent to begin with, then edit it every few months to keep it up to date.

Your listing is the first thing you should focus on because you can't launch your item without a listing – but it's not always the most important. You also need people to find your item.

Imagine Amazon was a giant store with tens of thousands of shelves.

You need to be able to lead customers to your shelf so they don't get lost, or just pick the first thing they see. Starting with a great listing is part of that – the package has to look good. People buy things based on the packaging and that's what your listing is, a nice pretty package to entice people into buying what you have.

In the next chapter, I'm going to show you how to lead people to that pretty package, so they can see your listing and buy your item.

Wondering If You Have A Million Dollar Listing?

Chat with us at +(512)-548-2467 and we can tell you if your listing is on track, plus help you build it bigger and better. My team and I would love to connect with you, so call us.

CHAPTER 14

MAKE YOURSELF DISCOVERABLE

"YOU CAN'T FIND what you want if you don't know what you're looking for."

> • *Matthew E. Fryer*

70% of the traffic to your Amazon listing comes from Amazon Mobile. Make sure your product listing looks good on a phone.

No, make sure your product listing looks great on a phone. On a tablet. On a computer. Everywhere. Once your listing is amazing, then reach out and make it more discoverable.

You want people to be able to find your listing, because if you don't, they won't.

Imagine you had a big store, like Walmart. There are thou- sands of shelves, with tens of thousands of products.

The products with the best shelf space, eye-level and in a good aisle, those are going to sell.

If you're not making your product discoverable on Amazon, then it's like your product is back in the storage part of Walmart. It's not even on a shelf. Nobody will see it, so nobody will buy it.

Here are some ways you can increase the number of people who find your product on Amazon.

Listing Optimization • Keyword Research

A Keyword is something that will show up in an Amazon search. If you're selling a yoga mat, you should put that it's a yoga mat somewhere in the clear, description. But you don't need to say it ten times. You have an entire product descrip- tion to add keywords into – not stuff. It should still make sense to anyone reading your product description.

Remember, if they've made it all the way to read your product description, they're much more likely to buy your item. They're already sold on the picture, the title, and the reviews. Now they want to read a little more about it to make sure it's what they want.

If you don't have words that people are typing when they want to buy a thing, it doesn't matter how good your thing is. No one's going to find you.

You can have the best pictures, the best price, the most amount of reviews. But if somebody goes and types yoga mat and you don't have yoga mat anywhere on the listing, no one's going to find you. They just won't.

This sounds very simple. It sounds very straightforward, yet so many people do not know how to use keywords. They don't do it. They don't practice it. Keyword research is very simple.

If you're not sure what keywords you should add, you can use a free tool like "Google Keyword Planner" to help search out good keywords that people are looking for. If I want to buy something, I want to just type it quickly into the search bar and have your product show up – because your listing has the keywords I typed in.

If I type in "Yoga mat for class," then those words should be in your listing somewhere.

Good Keyword Optimization: This ½" half-inch thick yoga mat is ideal for people of all ages who are looking for a non- slip, specialized mat that bundles up easily to take to class, or store it snugly when you get home with storage straps.

Bad Keyword Optimization: This is a yoga mat that's a yoga mat that people of all ages, kids, moms, dads, adults, seniors use to do yoga on the yoga mat. It's very yoga mat type of yoga mat and yoga yoga mat mat mat.

Pay Per Click Ads

• • •

If you are advertising your product, it's not any more important than your listing, and your listing is not more important than advertising.

What does that mean?

This is a real business. You need to get eyeballs looking at your product. It does require a little bit of extra effort, a little bit of action taken on your part.

PPC stands for pay-per-click. This is not as complicated. This is not the big, bad, scary, technical stuff that everybody makes this out to be.

I spend millions of dollars in advertising. I cannot run my Facebook or my Google ads. True story. I hire someone to do that. We still run our own PPC ads internally. They're easy.

This is very, very simple.

How much do you want to spend? You can either search for your own keywords or run an automatic campaign, where Amazon finds the best keywords for you. When you purchase PPC ads, Amazon sends traffic your way for people who they think are going to want to buy your thing. They get paid by you, because you pay for every click. If someone sees the ad and clicks your item, you pay a small fee for the advertising.

Now if you're paying for advertising, you want to make sure your listing is in order first. If you have a garbage listing that doesn't convert and doesn't make people want to buy your item, then you're wasting your money on advertising.

The advertising brings the right person to your item.

Your listing is what sells the item.

If someone searches for the keywords in your item, your listing should sell it.

If you pay-per-click for advertising, your listing should sell it.

Bigger ad spend is not going to save your listing if you didn't follow the formula and you didn't create a good item in the first place, or you didn't follow the formula and your listing doesn't have the required elements to sell.

Social Media

I crush the competition by utilizing social media.

So many people only rely on Amazon. The way Amazon works with PPC advertising is that there's a ceiling in how much traffic you can get. Based off of how much you spend per day, you can hit this ceiling.

However, there's only so much traffic the ads will bring

to your listing.

If I'm spending $300 per day and I'm profitable, but $300 is hitting the ceiling, I can't tell Amazon that I want to spend $3,000 a day. Because there just isn't enough volume for the customers who are on Amazon and see that PPC advertising.

There aren't enough searches.

Does that mean that it's the maximum capacity for your product? Does that mean that's the best that your product can do on Amazon?

No.

The best part of social media? It's absolutely free.

You can use this to generate more revenue and scale your business. You can create the accounts and put your stuff there so people can see it. You can reach out to other people who have audiences who can promote your stuff.

But people don't do it.

In November and December, around gifting season, we would create these blogs or these polls that we would put on Medium, and other blog sites like Reddit. I would say something like, "Top Christmas Gift of 2021 for Women," or "Top Giftable Item All Men Must Have in 2021."

It cost me nothing but an hour to write and post the article. And guess what? My items that I sell were those top giftable items.

Every single click that someone made when they read my article went directly to my product.

Amazon Associates Program

Amazon actually incentivizes you to bring exterior traffic onto Amazon.

It's called the Associates Program, and it's pretty easy to

sign up for.

When you bring traffic from somewhere else onto Amazon to buy your thing, chances are they're going to buy other things. You get paid a small bonus commission for your item, and anything else that customer buys. This is especially good for people who do their primary shopping on Amazon.

Chances are if they're not a prime member yet, they are going to fall in love with the greatest website in the world that has the fastest shipping, and best customer service, and they're going to become a Prime user.

Now, Amazon has made money off you. They've made money off the other products that they've sold. If person you linked wasn't already a Prime user and now they sign up for it, then Amazon is going to make more money.

You're going to make more money.

This is an easy program to sign up for, and if you're already going to the effort to bring in more customers to Amazon from other places, you need to sign up for it to make a ton of extra money.

You can even advertise items that you don't sell and make money when people click on them and buy them. But you will make even more leading people to your items because you make commission on the Associates Program and then you make money selling your item.

This will massively increase your profit. I know some people who make a full-time income on the Associates Program alone.

Reviews

• • •

Reviews are very, very important and massively underrated. It's the lifeblood of your listing. So many people focus on the price, the picture, the title, the quality, the advertising, and those are all absolutely essential – but they don't focus on reviews, and then they wonder why their stuff doesn't sell.

If you're searching for a restaurant to go eat at, would you eat at a place with no reviews?

No way.

If the restaurant had one, or two stars, would you eat there?

Nope.

I'm a star guy. If it ain't got 4.5, or 5 stars, I'm not going there. Especially if I'm traveling,I search out good food near me, or best food near me.

Pictures look good, food looks amazing. If it has no stars, I'm not eating there.

You absolutely need to get reviews for your product – lots of them, and good reviews, too. If you created a really good item, there's no reason why you should be getting a lot of bad reviews. A few are okay, they're legitimate. There are sad, lonely people out there that give Harry Potter a 1-star review. Shame on them, but they do it.

Your item should have a 4.5, or 5-star overall count for your reviews.

How do you get reviews? Ask.

Ask and ye shall receive.

Ask your friends, your neighbors. Offer to comp the item for them. Offer a freebie for an honest review. Ask customers who bought the item. Let them know that reviews are like gold, for sellers.

I always say it this way. "Do you love your new product? Please leave us an honest review! Anything we can fix so you're completely satisfied? Contact our customer service team so we can make it right."

People who love your item will leave a nice review. Anyone else can contact customer service so you can make it right and avoid any bad reviews.

There's no minimum number of reviews you should have before you start advertising and promoting your item, but zero is not okay. And 1, 2, or 3-star overall reviews are not okay.

You will get more reviews over time, especially if you followed the AMZ Formula and built an evergreen product that's going to last for a long time.

You can always go out and add more social media posts, more articles, and new, inventive ways to bring people to your Amazon listing. The most important part is to start the process now.

CHAPTER 15

BUILD IT

"IF YOU DON'T BUILD *your dream someone else will hire you to help build theirs."*

•*Tony Gaskins*

So far, I've focused the majority of this book on the mentality behind your own success, plus the online tools you need to list and promote your product.

You don't even have a product yet. That was completely intentional.

Until you've figured out your why, you shouldn't be working on your how.

I've told you that this is a marathon and not a sprint – but I also had to tell you which direction to go before you started running. If I started out with your product, you would be out there building it by yourself in your back yard or basement before you even knew what to build.

Yes, your product is absolutely one essential component of what you're selling with your online business. But it's not more important than your mindset, your listing, your advertising, or your reaching out and finding people to show the product to.

It's mutual. Without a product there would be no sale, no matter how good the other stuff was. With a product but no way of showing it to people or getting people to come see it, there would be no sale.

So yes, you do need to actually make something – or at least, you need to have someone make it for you. You didn't think this chapter was about woodworking, did you?

Here are the literal nuts and bolts of how to build a product for your Fulfillment By Amazon business.

Manufacturing Your Product

You want to get your product made, and you're going to need a lot of units. If you plan on selling a few hundred a day, you had better make a few thousand of these things. The worst feeling in the world is striking gold and running out of prod- uct, only to find it's going to take a few months to get more.

Can you imagine making $10,000 per day and then finding out there's no more of what you're selling? That's an expensive mistake. But you also don't want to find out you're making $10 per day and then you're sitting on a ton of unsold product.

Here are the three key steps to manufacturing your product so that you have something to sell.

1. Find the Product

Go back to the earlier chapters for tips on how to find a good product to launch. You want to break into a market that already has a lot of sales. Ideally, the price point for your item should be around $20 - $50. Look at the no-no list and do not start out making an item that's on that list.

2. Develop the Product

Scout around at all the competition and see what they're offering. Look at their good reviews to see what people love and include that in your product. Then look at their bad reviews to see what people dislike and change it. Offer something better. See if you can increase the price by offering a better value. Offer better design, better packaging, better bonuses, but do not decrease the price.

• • •

3. Find the Supplier

This is one of the trickiest steps. As I said before, you don't need to get a bunch of samples, or wait to hear back about quotes. Find the best manufacturer for your product. How? 7/10 times, goods made in China have high quality and the best price, but Taiwan has great factories. India and Bangla- desh have great textiles. Scout your competition to see where they're making their products. They're legally required to say.

How to Find A World-Class Supplier

There's more to finding the supplier than just doing an internet search. Here are some key goodies on making sure you're going with the best company for making your product.

The following five features define a great supplier for your product. To me, communication is key, but every single one of these elements are important.

1. Rating

• • •

You can almost always find what a supplier has already made on their website. You can also use a site called www.Alibaba.com to find ratings for every supplier in China. It's like looking at the back end of Amazon – you can just see user reviews and ratings for what it was like to work with that company. There are some really amazing companies out there, so make sure you pick a winner.

Track Record

You want to know how long it's estimated before your product will take, and how good it will be. You can do research on a company or ask them. How long have they been in business? What's their commitment to quality? How many employees do they have? How much revenue have they generated? What's their return policy, if any?

Communication

Communication is huge. Why? Because if you can't get in contact with them, you can't have a conversation with them. If they never respond to you, you can't order any product. Once you find the right product, you find a great supplier, they make the product for you, and you're making money on it – you have to make sure they can continue to make the product so you can keep selling it. You have to make sure that you guys are on the same page. It's one of my most important things when reaching out to the supplier, not price. Remember to be respectful of time differences, cultural differ- ences, and language barriers.

Capacity

If your product is selling like hotcakes and you're making $10,000 profit a month, and you run out of product. You want to know what capacity your supplier can produce for you. How many and how fast? Especially if you have a great first run and you're ready to order more, you want to know how quickly you can replenish your stock. Additionally, bigger manufacturers often offer discount if you order in massive volume. You might not want to do that at first, but if you're selling very well, then you can make even more money by offering to buy in volume, which will often decrease the price.

Quality

You get what you pay for, and quality is something you should be prepared to buy. You want a supplier who can make you the best quality items out there. This is worth your money because it will always show in your end product, no matter how clever the design or pretty the packaging. Apple doesn't just build epic boxes to ship their computers in – there has to be a high-quality machine inside to stay at the top.

Compare Yourself To Others

Rather, you want to compare your products to other people's products.

You can actually ask your manufacturer about your competitors' products.

You can ask them what the quality difference is between yours and all the other competitors. They'll tell you exactly. They might say, "They use better garments. They use better material. They use thicker boxes. They use better paint. They don't use stickers. They use enamel."

They will tell you, but you have to ask. Ask and ye shall receive.

If they're doing something good, then make sure you're doing something good.

Then do it better.

Use Specialists
• • •

I love specialists.

They're expensive, but I love them.

If you want special results, which are results that other people are not getting, you have to do things that others are not doing.

If everybody is focused on saving money and they're all racing to the bottom, competing on low prices, you will not dominate the competition, flourish to the top and make more than everybody else when you're simply mimicking them. Fighting them to the bottom on that price war is not profitable for anybody and it's a race that everyone loses.

To make a special product, seek out a specialist that can help you make that product.

Pay more, so you can make more.

You do the finding of the product, the creative part where you think about how you can add on to this product and make it better.

You do the work of finding the supplier, the manufacturer, or the specialist.

Then you coast.

You let the manufacturer make things and ship them to Amazon.

You let Amazon store those things and ship them directly to customers when they're ordered.

You let Amazon cut you a check at the end of the month for everything you've sold.

Congratulations, you have yourself a business.

CHAPTER 16

BUILD IT BETTER

"IF OPPORTUNITY DOESN•T KNOCK, build a door."
•Milton Berle

I've changed a lot since I was younger.

In many ways, I've become wiser and obviously, I've become older. But honestly, it's only in the last five years I really became introspective and looked at who I was.

I was in a bad situation, with a terrible job that didn't even pay the rent. But truthfully, no matter how bad the hand I was dealt, it was still up to me for never changing myself. I was committed to living an impoverished life and I accepted my circumstances, thinking I might just get ahead if I worked more hours.

I wasn't even a very good employee at the recycling center because my heart wasn't in it. It was when I recog- nized that if I wanted to change my situation, I had to change myself, that I finally was able to take accountability for who I really was.

I had a terrible job because I didn't have the skills for anything else.

I didn't have the skills for anything else because I wasn't really paying attention.

There are opportunities all around us. Everywhere. All of us. Tons of them.

I realized I needed to become better so I could do better, and earn better.

If you are not operating in excellence, you are compromising.

I was tired of compromising. I had to build a better me, to build a better system for earning my living.

When the pain of who I was, was too much for me to live through, I changed.

When the pain of not making enough money to support myself and my family was too much of a burden for me to bear, I changed.

And I have never looked back.

If you can build it, like you did in the last chapter, you can build it better.

Build yourself better, build your idea better, build your product better.

Zig Zag

• • •

Zig Ziglar is one of the greatest marketers of our generation.

He said that when the market zigs you zag. That means you do the complete opposite of everybody else. If you want results that others are not getting, is it logical to do what others are doing and expect anything different?

No.

Be different, be better, get better results.

Start looking where nobody else is looking. What is the rest of the market missing that you can find if you look a little longer? A little deeper? A little differently?

Everything on Amazon sells, but you have to ask the questions inside of the AMZ Formula for success. You have to answer those questions yourself, and you have to answer them differently than everyone else.

There's a yoga mat that's crushing the market?

Everyone jumps to launch a blue yoga mat, or a red one, that's identical in every other way.

No.

You're going to create frown lines on your customers faces if you just go with the same old item they've seen on Amazon a thousand other times.

The market launches their yoga mats all the same, but different colors – you offer a different material, a sustainable rubber slip-proof mat that has a handle, plus neat straps for storage, a carry tote to put it in, multiple colors including shiny rose gold, two balance bricks and a yoga ball.

You zag, create a better product, something useful. Then you charge more and crush the competition.

Monetize The Back

Amateurs monetize the front end and experts monetize the back.

When you are negotiating with your suppliers, do not drive down the quality of your packaging in order to increase your profits.

Customer service.

You guys want to do something else creative after today? Write this down, you guys can do it after the event. Go into your orders, look at something you've bought, click on their store and see what type of customer support they have. See the cool thing is Amazon handles customer support for us. They handle the returns, they handle all of that stuff. However, do you think of the offer customer support outside of waiting online to talk to somebody at Amazon, it would be beneficial to your business. Any of you guys ever shop with a company or go to a restaurant or go somewhere to do busi- ness with somebody and you loved their product, you loved their food, but number five was off and you never did busi- ness with them again?

Customer service, a very high percentage of Amazon sellers do not have external customer service. When I started in 2014, there was a company by the name of grasshopper for

$19, you could have a phone number, that's a business phone number, that comes in through your cell phone because I had no money for a business line and customers could call me and it would come to my phone. Hi, thank you for calling Josh's brand customer service. How can I help you? I was the owner. I was the CEO. I was everything. And I was acting like customer service, but guess what? They were shocked. Wow, you have a customer service.

We're a small family owned business and we really want to take care of our customers. We pride ourselves in being the best at what we do and offering the best customer service. How many of you guys think I was crushing the competi- tion? How many you guys think that if you did something like that, it doesn't have to be you picking up the phone. Like, come on Josh, you told me I ain't going to have to, why are you talking about answering the phone and customer support? You don't have to do it, but you can hire a VA to do it for $3 an hour.

And you don't even have to have a phone line. Just have an email on there. Support at Joshsbrandgmail.com, support at Joshsbrand.com. Most sellers don't even have that. You got to communicate through the seller dashboard. Anything that you can do to go above and beyond what your competition is doing is going to work to your advantage.

Because in order to get results at other peoples they're not getting, you have to do what others are not doing.

• • •

How to Scale Your Business

Amateurs monetize the front end and experts monetize the back. Here are some tried and true techniques for scaling your business bigger.

Do not try this on your first item, or when you're first starting out.

But when you've experienced some success and you feel like you're getting the hang of it, then go ahead and try these five steps for increasing your presence, and your profit.

1. Order More Inventory

Once you realize that your product is selling well, the first thing is to order more inventory. This is partly so you don't get stuck with a product that's selling great, but then suddenly sold out of inventory. The beautiful thing about ordering more inventory, is that your supplier will often give you price breaks for high-volume orders. Obviously, you need to order enough inventory so you don't run out of supplies. If you start scaling your advertising and sales, but miss this step, then you could be earning zero on your product when it's sold out. This can create a happy circle for you, because if you get your product for less, you can decrease your price (only then!) which will sell more volume, which will in turn allow you to order more inventory.

• • •

2. Increase Your Advertising Budget

It takes money to make money. You have to order the inventory and then sell it to make a profit. You have to buy ads if you want to sell a lot of that inventory. Yes, you can sell some things and do okay without spending money on ads. Eventually, you will sell out of your inventory and need to order more. But why wait for eventually? Why sell 10 prod- ucts a day with no ad spend when you can sell 100 products a day and spend a few dollars on ads? There's an author who sells over $1 million dollars per year of his own books on Amazon. He spends about $600 thousand dollars on adver- tising to reach those figures. Do you think he's bummed to be spending that much, when his income is over $400 thousand dollars per year? Spend the money, even if it's uncomfortable.

3. Increase Your Advertising Strategy

You can also advertise your items off Amazon. Instagram, Facebook, Google Ads. Find out where your customers are and buy more advertising there. You want to try everything to bring people to where you are. This is an advanced tech- nique, so only try this after you've already capped your Amazon Ad spending.

• • •

4. Use Working Capital & Credit.

OPM is the best solution for buying your products in the first place. That's Other People's Money. Borrow money from a low-interest lender, or even get a credit card that offers rewards, and no or low interest for paying it back. Get a miles card and earn enough miles to take your family on a nice vacation. Amazon even has a system called Amazon working capital. They will incentivize you to grow your business and make more money, because when you win, they win. When you start a business with Amazon, you are partnering with one of the largest companies in the world. You are partnering with the richest man alive. He makes money, when you make money. If you make more money, he makes more money. If you have a good credit and you're starting a business, start a business credit card. You can use 100% of the limit that you have on your business credit card. If you lack resources, become resourceful. If you want to get to the next level, become resourceful.

The successful all leverage credit. They all leverage debt. When you have debt that earns money instead of subtracts from your net worth, or from the amount of money that you make, it is called positive debt. That's how you create cash flow using OPM.

• • •

5. Vertically Integrate

One of the easiest ways to scale is to offer a new variation of your product. Why do so many people, when they want to scale, they want to make more money, they want to grow their business, they go and they find another product to sell, something completely different? Beats by Dre only sells head- phones. It's a multiple eight figure per year company, and they only sell expensive headphones. Do you know how many variations of headphones they have? They don't offer the Beats by Dre home gym or meal plan because nobody wants that. They sell tons of different types of expensive headphones and that's it. Learn from Dre. Keep it simple. Sell the same thing, just a little different.

More Ideas For Scaling

I didn't want to just give you ten ideas for scaling your

business at once, because these are different. These ideas for making your business bigger come after you tried those last five. And those last five come after you've already experienced some success with selling your products.

It should go without saying that these advanced tactics for scaling are only for people who really know what they're doing.

Ignore that last piece of advice at your own risk. Here are five more creative ways you can get bigger and reach a wider audience.

Sustained Previous Products

Never abandon your first flow. Never abandon your first product. Just because a product is working, don't just move on to another product and never make the first one better. Maybe you were almost onto something but missed a key detail, or maybe it just wasn't the right time. Once you exhaust that product and it's earning revenue, that product is running like a machine. It's a cash cow making you money every single day, every single week, every single month. Make sure that you go back and check up on that thing. If you take care of your asset, your asset will take care of you.

Add to Your Catalog

The easiest way to scale is to vertically integrate, like I pointed out in that last batch of techniques. But after you exhaust your advertising, after you exhaust the opportunity to build different variations of the same thing, now it's time to add to your catalog and horizontally integrate. Vertical inte- gration is adding accessories, improving, and making it better. Horizontal integration is when you add additional products to your catalog, or go into different industries.

Beats by Dre made Dre a fortune. But he also made excellent albums and made a fortune. The key here is exhausting your opportunity first, then moving on to something new.

business at once, because these are different. These ideas for making your business bigger come after you tried those last five. And those last five come after you've already experienced some success with selling your products.

It should go without saying that these advanced tactics for scaling are only for people who really know what they're doing.

Ignore that last piece of advice at your own risk. Here are five more creative ways you can get bigger and reach a wider audience.

Sustained Previous Products

Never abandon your first flow. Never abandon your first product. Just because a product is working, don't just move on to another product and never make the first one better. Maybe you were almost onto something but missed a key detail, or maybe it just wasn't the right time. Once you exhaust that product and it's earning revenue, that product is running like a machine. It's a cash cow making you money every single day, every single week, every single month. Make sure that you go back and check up on that thing. If you take care of your asset, your asset will take care of you.

Add to Your Catalog

The easiest way to scale is to vertically integrate, like I pointed out in that last batch of techniques. But after you exhaust your advertising, after you exhaust the opportunity to build different variations of the same thing, now it's time to add to your catalog and horizontally integrate. Vertical inte- gration is adding accessories, improving, and making it better. Horizontal integration is when you add additional products to your catalog, or go into different industries.

Introduce New Products & Brands

You can introduce new products and new brands into the market you're already selling in. You can be Coke and Pepsi, if you want to. That's a metaphor, because Coke and Pepsi are intellectual copyright, so you can't actually be them. But there's no rule on Amazon that says you can't own competing brands in the same industry. I always suggest you start with one. Then if that's already successful and you've exhausted your opportunity there, create another item in the same industry but change a few things. Change the brand, the design, the price, the add-ons, the bundle. Now you're dominating the market because customers are choosing between you, or you.

Look For Additional Options

See where you can find and add additional options. Look for ways of new advertising, new partnerships, new brands, new niches, new industries, new variations. Try an improved version of your product, or a new model, or a different size. Keep your original one rocking, but launch another one. Always be adding. You can start by specializing in Queen beds until you've mastered that. Then add full, twin, King, California King. You don't have to do everything when you're first starting out, but now that you've gotten somewhere and had some sales and have some traction, always be on the lookout for additional options.

Exhaust

Exhaust anything and everything that you do. You want to squeeze the lemon dry to make lemonade, carve it out, make lemon merengue pie, chop up the peel and use the zest. Use the seeds and grow them into more lemon trees. You want to take every opportunity you have and really, truly, try absolutely everything before moving on. You put the hard work up front, lots of it, tons of it, cherish the work, love what you do, take massive action – and you will be rewarded with a successful item. Why? Because nobody else is doing that. They take a lemon and throw it at the wall to see if it's juicy. Then they throw another lemon. Once you exhaust all your opportunities to improve, add and be creative, then you can take a nice well-deserved break because your item will be successful.

• • •

Build It With Us

Give us a call at +(512)-548-2467 and you might be surprised at how much we can help you take off and keep progressing. It's what we do – teach people to be better and better so they can make more money by building a bigger online presence. We would love to chat.

CHAPTER 17

CREATING YOUR NEXT PRODUCT

"MONEY WON'T CREATE SUCCESS, *the freedom to make it will."*

— Nelson Mandela

You now have the ultimate guide for how to launch your own Fulfilment By Amazon online business.

You have the tools, the strategy, the wisdom and hopefully, you also have the motivation to actually go out and do it.

But it's not just about getting lucky with one single item. It's possible, but unlikely that you will nail this on your first try.

Luck favors the prepared, so get prepared.

Be prepared to put in a lot of hard work on the front end so you can relax and enjoy more time and hours of your life on the back end.

Be prepared to swerve and change your offering, your list- ing, your ads, your traffic.

This may seem very obvious, but be prepared to create another product. And then another. And then another.

For me, it took me a few mistakes that I learned from before I came up with my profitable item. I'm glad I didn't give up after three tries because three tries was not a charm for me. It was my fourth item that struck gold and started earning me five figures per month.

I still had the other three items and kept selling a little bit of those, too.

I didn't stop just because I had one golden goose. I kept listing things.

I followed my own formula and kept listing things until I was bringing in six figures per year, and then six figures per month!

If you're the rare type of individual who's going to read this book and take action on it, I applaud you. Good for you. Change your life.

But don't stop.

Keep making stuff, keep creating, keep listing on Amazon and build your empire.

Putting It All Together
• • •

If you're confused about any of the steps to creating your own FBA business, go back through this book and read those chapters again. Read the whole book again. Take notes. Go through it until you get it.

Each step is part of the formula. There are no shortcuts.

If you're making a cake and you remove a cup of flour, or take away one of the eggs, the recipe is going to be a disaster. The cake is no good if you don't follow the recipe.

If you bake a thousand cakes and they all come out great

and then you want to get experimental, go ahead – you earned that privilege.

Don't mess with the recipe for success that the AMZ Formula offers you. Every step of it is designed to save you the heartbreak of losing time and money from launching products that suck and don't sell.

If you would like step by step tutorials, motivation, more specifics and a host of other really powerful online business builders on exactly what I've covered in this book, then I urge you to come join us for my online course at https://www. theamzformula.com/

This is the exact program that I've used to work with and watch thousands of students from over 100 countries to create and grow their online businesses. My top twenty students alone have sold over a billion dollars' worth of their own products. I like to show you exact numbers by sharing my screen and literally checking my Amazon account balance so you can see that everything I'm telling you is true.

I've found that people are often looking for a little nudge to get off their easy chair and take action. This is it. Investing in yourself (the course is practically free compared to how much you will earn once you go through it) is the best thing you can do for your own personal growth.

We have plenty of bonuses, freebies and extras for people who take action and join us. I hope to see you there.

Scale Your Business

You built one product?

Great! Now it will be even easier to launch your next product, and your next.

You can kick back and relax after you've launched a golden goose that brings you in a comfortable living, or you can keep scaling your business and grow it bigger.

You will always get out of something what you put into it, so make sure you stay on top of managing and optimizing your listing and keywords so that you can keep your evergreen products selling well.

Then create more.

Use the knowledge and experience that you personally gain from successfully launching your first few products to build up – and to build sideways.

You launched a yoga mat? (I really hope you didn't do that).

Now launch a yoga ball. And a yoga balance brick.

Now package all three of those items as a complete set and offer a yoga package for beginners. (Please, please don't actually do that. This is just an example of what you can do).

The only limitation to how big you can grow your company is you. So get out there and build it!

Your Network Determines Your Net Worth

Have you ever quit drinking and you found out that some of your friends only hung out with you because you were drinking buddies?

If you're ready to radically change your ways, your income, your business, and your lifestyle, you might find that you outgrow some of your friends.

Now some of your homies are friends for life, so I'm not saying that you should ever abandon them. But some people that still have that poverty mentality, or fixed mindset, or self-limiting beliefs – those might not be your people anymore.

Especially once you get wealthy, you're going to have a lot of people hitting you up for money.

If someone hits you up for money, you hand them a copy of this book and let them know they can make as much money as they want with the AMZ Formula.

You need to find people a community of people who support you. People with the same dreams. Growth-minded people with a vision.

I don't want to sound elite at all, but you need to find other winners who believe in you.

I had to leave some of my friends behind when I got successful and I tell you something true – I don't really miss them. I absolutely brought my homies with me. I showed my close friends exactly what I was doing with Amazon and they came right along with me and became successful.

It's not about the money – it's about the mentality.

At the AMZ Formula, we have a pretty tight-knit group of people that do the same thing – we grow. We're committed. We lift each other up.

We know each other's struggles so we can relate. But we don't commiserate and stay down. We find ways to dig deeper and build bigger.

That's my group of friends now and some of my homies are a part of it. You can find us in a Facebook group that's limited to people who have been through the AMZ Formula online course. I'm not trying to sell you on a course, I'm trying to sell you on an entire lifestyle shift.

Instead of trying to out-bad your friends and complain about who has to work more hours or has a worse boss, you can chat with your friends about which properties you have your eye on to buy next, or where your next vacation is for you and your family. I recommend the Maldives – not because it's pretentious, but because it's mind-blowingly beautiful and it changed my life swimming in the blue-green water there.

Join Our Network And Increase Your Net Worth

• • •

Call us at +(512)-548-2467 and join our team. I'm not the only one making an extremely comfortable and full-time living from selling on Amazon. If you really want to change who you're talking to, I just offered you the option of talking to us, so we can grow together.

CHAPTER 18

FINDING A MENTOR

"IF YOU EVER FIND THAT *you're the most talented person in the room, you need to find another room."*

•*Austin Kleon*

My entire life and the lives of everyone around me changed for two reasons.

First, I was ready to change. I wanted out of my old lifestyle that wasn't working. I wanted a better life for myself and my family. I didn't want to die in debt, so I made a commitment to myself that I was going to take action and change it. I was going to build a fortune for myself so I wasn't working a dead-end job until I died.

It always starts on the inside. Nobody can make you change. It's all you.

Second, I found a mentor. Or my mentor found me. Either way, a good mentor will take their years of experience and knowledge, then transfer that to you. You can always do it without a mentor, but you might have to repeat their count- less wasted hours and thousands, or even millions of dollars in mistakes.

Would Luke Skywalker have ever become a Jedi Knight if he didn't meet his mentor, old Obi-Wan Kenobi in the desert? Maybe, but maybe not. The Empire torched his farm and killed his entire family looking for him just minutes after he left on his quest, and he definitely wasn't ready for that yet. He would probably just be another dead farmer in the desert, living up to the expectations of society that he was never going to amount to anything. Just another news story about poor people who died doing poor people things.

I want you to take action now.

NOW means No Opportunity Wasted.

It's a growth mindset where you use all of your resources. Keep looking. Keep searching. Keep discovering how vast a universe is out there and what a small microcosm you are.

If you're ready to grow bigger and have a larger sphere of influence over your life and the rest of the world then you need to take action now, and leave no opportunity wasted.

Get yourself a good mentor.

What You Can Get From A Mentor
• • •

When you're ready to grow, get out there and find yourself a mentor, whether it's someone who wrote a book that changed your life, or an in-person or on-zoom meeting with someone you can respect because they know what the heck they're talking about.

You should choose someone who has been on the path that you're on – and succeeded. Don't settle for a mentor who knows a little bit about what you want to know about. These days there are some people who call them- selves experts when they're really only one step ahead of you.

That's not a mentor. You follow that person's footsteps and they might lead you right off a cliff.

Like a good sports coach, a good mentor can take you

further, faster. They can help you grow. They can identify something unique and beautiful inside of you and draw that thing out. They can help you achieve things you've never dreamed possible.

I've personally mentored a number of people who wanted to do what I do. I taught them everything I know, but mentoring is more than teaching. I legitimately saw each of these people for who they are and helped them capitalize on their own strengths.

I also created a team of mentors to help people like you grow their Amazon businesses bigger, faster.

Some people come to us because they're lost and need more hands-on training to do it. They succeed. They do it in their own way, with our help.

Some people come to us because they want to get really big, really fast. They succeed. They do it their own way, with our help.

Sometimes people want to have the ideas and hire us to help them do everything else – to contact the suppliers, set up the listing. We do that too. If you know you have a million- dollar idea and you want to hire a team of experts to help you make that come to life, that's completely legit. We have done that and seen some amazing results.

But this isn't for everyone. We actually have an application process for anyone looking to get mentoring from us. It's the kind of thing that builds a very successful business very quickly, but only the right people will benefit from it.

This is not because we're exclusive – we have Black people, Hispanic people, white people, Asian people, all kinds of people who apply and get in because they're committed to their business, and to themselves. We also reject even more people because they're wishy-washy and I don't want to waste their money getting wishy-washy results.

If you think you're ready to take massive action and get

personal help on every element of building and growing your Amazon business, then you can apply at www.amzapply. com

We're here waiting to help create the next success story.

Why Mentors Give Back

As people age, we discover that there's much more to the world than just money.

When we're constantly struggling to pay bills and keep our head above water, it seems like money is the only important thing because it's the only thing we can focus on. Once money is removed from the equation because there's plenty of it, we can focus on more essential things like pondering the meaning of our existence.

No matter how rich you get, millionaire, billionaire, we are all human and we all still struggle with the same philosophical questions at the end of the day.

What comes after I die? What will I leave behind?

True, genuine, lasting happiness does not come from money. You might think that right now, but that's not the case. Once you have your bills paid, a nice place to live, and everything you could ever want, you find out there's a lot more to life.

Giving to others offers you a sense of purpose, which will create a lasting sense of happiness.

This is something I discovered a few years back, and it changed my life completely. It was my second transformation.

My first life shift was when I went from nobody making minimum wage, to owning my own business and being wealthier than anyone I knew. It was a huge success story for me and it brought my family and I a lot of comfort – but not lasting happiness.

Being able to show others how to replicate my success

and bring themselves out of debt, out of poverty, and finally have free time to spend doing what they love and being with their families has made me incredibly grateful.

I now have a sense of purpose that's better than anything else in my life, save being a good husband and good father.

This is something I want to share with you if you're willing to join me on a journey to create a massively successful life for you.

Your Legacy

When you die, what will people say about you?

What will your kids say about you when they're standing over your grave?

"That was a dad who drank a lot of beer and watched a lot of Netflix. He worked really hard, and we will be working really hard to pay for this funeral."

Wow. Or maybe, "That was a mom who always wanted to take us to Disneyland. She never did, but it's sweet that she always meant to. We sold her wedding ring to pay for this funeral."

You're better than that. You're somebody.

Maybe nobody has believed in you before. Maybe you've never believed in yourself before.

Well there's nobody who's magically going to do it now unless you start the process.

As Steve Martin said, "Be so good they can't ignore you."

Go out and take action now. Today. This moment.

Become somebody special by working for it, not wishing for it.

When you set this book down, I want you to do something, anything, to prove to yourself that change is possible – because it is.

I leave you on that note.

God bless,

Joshua Crisp

PS. You're only one product away! If you want to know what to do next so you can start this for real, call us at +(512)-548-2467

BONUS CASE STUDIES - THE REAL DEAL

The AMZ Formula wouldn't be a formula if it didn't work for everyone – or at least everyone who put in the effort to follow the formula step by step.

These are three real examples of students of mine who studied with me, used the AMZ Formula to launch their own businesses in their own way, and came out massively success- ful. Their entire lives changed.

With their permission, they've allowed me to print their stories so that you can see that I'm not just a lucky guy who accidentally got rich. I'm a lucky guy who got rich by using a proven formula that worked for me, worked for them, and will work for you.

Joseph

Before I got into selling on Amazon, I had the worst job in the world.

That was my number one motivation to get into Amazon and create my own business for myself.

I had this alcoholic boss. He would swear at me every day in the office, it was just a terrible situation. I was living in a one bedroom apartment, renting for like $400 bucks a month and I could barely afford that. For me, opening up a business on Amazon had to work because I had no other way out. I knew that job wasn't going to last very long.

Just like anyone that has a big problem in their life, I was asking for financial help. I went to family members and everyone told me, "Well, you should work for the post office because up here in the Northeast, you can get in with a union and you'll be all set the rest of your life."

I did not want to work for the post office. That was not my thing. I had to do something else because I wanted to make money where I could afford a house one day. I wanted to make enough money so that I could have a family one day. And there was really no other way.

So when I got into opening up an online business with Amazon, I was just thinking about selling used things online. I was making like a few hundred bucks a month, a thousand dollars here, but it wasn't sustainable because I was going out every night after work, on the weekends, just hustling. I was doing more work at my current job trying to keep that up. And then thankfully I found Josh from the AMZ Formula on Instagram and I got ahold of him and I learned about Amazon and I got into the private label business model.

The difference between then and now is so massive. Honestly, back then I could never think of me being here. Owning a home, remodeling, having a huge business, selling over a hundred units a day. It's just crazy. I could never have dreamed that I would have all this in my life because I never thought that highly of myself.

But it's not about that, it's about learning. It's about figuring these numbers out like Josh showed me. And if you can write it out, if you can set these goals, if you can have the right mindset and know that you have to work in order for this business to succeed, you can have success too.

Believe me, I was at the same spot as I'm sure a lot of you are in right now. There's no way out. But, if you're willing to do the work, I'm living proof. I did it and I'm not a super smart guy. I never got A's in high school. So if I can do it, you guys can do it too.

Eileen

First and foremost, I'm very thankful for a mentor like Joshua and even a friend-tor like Joey, you can't be around these guys and work around these guys and not be great.

When I started with Joshua, I knew nothing about Amazon. And even though this day, I sit here before you, I know the thing, the secret, but I love so much what I do working with him and working behind the scenes with people who come to us for help.

I invested in the AMZ Formula for myself, to help give me free time.

I am a single mom. My son just turned five. For those of you that have little ones, you know how it can be. My son is my why I do what I do. I do it for him.

So you can't be around these guys and be involved in the AMZ Formula and not be great.

Secondly, my son is the one that just drives me to do everything. And this was a way for me to secure a future for him and start generational wealth for his kids and their kids, and so on, and so forth.

My business has been up and running for not even a full

year yet. I believe next month is a year. I am already getting ready to cross that six figure mark.

It's a huge accomplishment for myself, and I'm very proud. You know, things kind of hit different before I was working with Josh.

All I did was retail management at my former career, but that first month that I was involved in the AMZ Formula and had my own product, my paycheck hit and I looked at it, and I said, "Wow, I made more sales and profit in this one month with my product selling while other people are managing everything for me, then I made in an entire year working hard hours at retail management the year my son was born."

More in one month than one year of me slaving. And I didn't even work 40 hours a week on my Amazon store.

It was crazy, insane, but enough about me.

I see that we help others all the time. Everybody has a different reason, a different outcome of what it is that they want to achieve or accomplish.

To me, it's a great honor to be behind the scenes, working to help shape people's dreams, goals, desires and watch them come true.

It's just truly amazing. And I see it happen over and over again for others. I see it and I get happy every time.

But when it happens for you, it kind of hits a little different, like woo. But that's it. That's my story.

Neil

There's a funny thing that Josh says, and I tell people this all the time. One of the most important things you will ever do in life is invest in yourself.

And the funny thing, when I'm explaining this to people, people are thinking I'm saying that it means you're supposed to invest in a course, or a mentor.

Most people won't do anything with the information

or advice anyway. More importantly, they just feel excited about the information anyway. They just feel excited about the current feeling, but they're never willing to do anything about it.

But let me tell you the cool thing. In the last two years, I personally invested $225,000 in my personal development. I don't know what your ethnicity is, reader, but every room that I go in, I'm often one of the only African-Americans in the room.

I came to realize the reason why I am the only person of my ethnicity in the room and the reason why I'm advancing is because I'm the guy who decided to take a chance and bet on myself.

That's the problem with so many of us. We keep doing the same thing over and over and over again, and somehow expecting different results. And then we never get different results. And we're trying to figure out, why is life remaining the same?

Have you been doing the same thing over and over again, but now you are ready for different results?

When I'm in these rooms and I'm realizing like, yo, why are none of my other Black brothers and Black sisters in the room? Why aren't we advancing? Why aren't we getting to that next level?

I've come to realize that anytime is a good time for us to invest in ourselves. Anytime, it's time for us to bet on ourselves and what BET stands for is Become Everything Today.

We never bet on ourselves. We never make a decision to do better. Then we wonder why everybody else around us advancing. So as I continue to collect the awards, as I continue to shatter different records, I realize that the reason why we're doing this is because we're putting it all on the line.

One of the things that I know is true is that when you're willing to go to that next level, you're going to have to give up some things. I tell people all the time, what are you willing to give up in order to go up?

What are you personally willing to give up in order to go up?

I want you to personally think about this. Get deep. What are you willing to let go? What are you willing to shed?

I was willing to give up the old me. I was willing to give up some of my money. I was willing to give up this old way of thinking, I was willing to give up a scarcity mentality. And I was willing to dig deep.

When they build skyscrapers, they have to lay the founda- tion deep. The deeper they dig, the more they add to the foundation, the

I've been to 55 countries in the world. And I was so amazed at the number one tallest building in the world, which at the time was the Burj Khalifa. But it dawned on me that in order for them to build the tallest building in the world, how big, how deep do you think they have to dig?

They have to dig deeper than they would normally dig for building a regular house. Building a skyscraper like that is going to take more effort, more energy. But the deeper they dig, the higher they can go up.

I've been a guy building my foundation over the years. I've been the guy willing to dig deeper to build higher. I know the deeper I go, the higher I'm going to be able to elevate and reach new levels.

I'm very clear that despite me giving you this information, despite what you've read in the rest of this book, only a very small percentage of you at best is probably going to take advantage of the opportunity to change your lives, dig deeper, and build something amazing.

Whether you invest in an online Amazon business or whether you investing yourself, you have to make a decision to dig deeper, you got to make a decision to make this your year.

So many of you are doing everything for everyone else, for your kids. You're doing everything for your parents. You're doing everything for everybody around you. But when was the last time you did anything for you? When you said "Now is my time. Now is my time to make a decision."

Today is the day that you can make a decision to better yourself. Get motivated. Leave a legacy for your family. Be the person who changes the game.

This decision might scare you. It might feel selfish. You might feel like you don't deserve it.

To me, I want my money to work for me and not me to constantly be working for my money. Cash is trash unless it is used. Every dollar that sit in my bank account is not working for me. I'm losing out. Everything that I do right now. I've leveraged all of my money. My money must be working for me. Your money needs to be your employee.

If your money is not working for you, if it's just sitting in a fractional reserve account, making one penny, two pennies a month, you are doing a disservice to your money. And you're also not only doing a disservice to your money, you're doing a disservice to your future.

Most people and their kids are not evolving, not doing great. Your kids are looking at you not doing great. They're looking at you making the decision to settle, every single day. They're looking at you making the decision to live an average life. You're role modeling mediocrity for them.

FEAR stands for Finally Exiting an Average Reality. If you're thinking of investing in yourself, but you're afraid, that's okay. I understand that. But how many years are you going to not try? How many years are going to go by and you're still exactly where you are right now? Just older.

Be honest with yourself. What are you willing to give up in order to go up?

I'm from the hood. I used to live paycheck to paycheck. My friends around me went to jail. They got kicked out of high school, kicked out of college, fired from jobs. I'm not okay with that cycle repeating for my kids, and I'm not okay with being broke. I'm not leaving my kids in debt when I die. My number one role model is Sam Walton. His children are the 16th, 17th, 18th, and 19th, wealthiest people in the world. And they have been in the top twenty since he died 30 years ago.

That's generational wealth.

Now that you've read this book and found out there's a different way to exist, a life you can live that's so different and so much better, what are you going to do about it? Are you going to get excited, but not change? Or, are you going to join the rest of us that dug a deep foundation, built something great, and lived a better life for ourselves and for our children?

I hope you're not okay with going to your old way of life now that you know something different is possible.

What's Next?

You've read the book. You've read the testimonials. If you made it this far, I'm guessing you're ready to do this. If you have any questions, please call me at +(512)-548-2467 and I can help you figure out what the next step is.

Let's do this!

ABOUT THE AUTHOR

Joshua Crisp is an author, entrepreneur and real estate mogul. In only five years, he went from making minimum wage at a recycling plant to scaling his own Fulfillment By Amazon business up to seven figures. He has since developed the AMZ Formula online training series, helping thousands of students from over 100 countries to successfully follow in his footprints and create their own profitable Fulfillment By Amazon businesses. His educational coaching program Crisp Learning Technologies is a community for growth-minded individuals who want to scale their business bigger and better. He and his dozens of employees offer turnkey opera- tions and a-la-carte solutions for people looking to build their Amazon businesses.

RESOURCES

Have questions or Need Help?
Text me lets chat 512-548-2467

Schedule a call with my team at www.1productawaycall.com

Save Money On The Software We Use To Find Winning Products!
www.discountonjunglescout.com

Learn about working with me and my team as a client where we
help you build or build you a Amazon business www.amztogether.com

Lets Connect :

Instagram: www.instagram.com/officialjoshuacrisp
Twitter: www.twitter.com/iamjoshuacrisp
Facebook: www.facebook.com/jcrispmarketing
Tik Tok: www.tiktok.com/@officialjoshuacrisp
Website: www.officialjoshuacrisp.com